A HISTORY OF
BRITISH BUS SERVICES
North East

A HISTORY OF
BRITISH BUS SERVICES
North East

DAVID HOLDING

DAVID & CHARLES
Newton Abbot   London   North Pomfret (Vt)

To My Wife

whose dislike of the omnibus was equalled only by her
tolerance while I was writing this book.

British Library Cataloguing in Publication Data

Holding, David
    A history of British bus services, North East.
    1. Motor bus lines — England — History
    I. Title
    388.3'22'09428   HE5664.N/

ISBN 978-1-4463-0654-3

Library of Congress Catalog Card Number 79-52370

© DAVID HOLDING 1979

Typeset by Northern Phototypesetting Co., Bolton
Printed in Great Britain by
Redwood Burn Ltd., Trowbridge and Esher
for David & Charles (Publishers) Limited
Brunel House, Newton Abbot, Devon

Published in the United States of America
by David & Charles Inc.
North Pomfret, Vermont 05053, USA

CONTENTS

FOREWORD

I am delighted to contribute this introduction to Mr Holding's interesting and colourful history of bus and coach operation in North-East England. The variety and extent of bus operation in the area probably exceeds that provided in most other areas of Great Britain, and Mr Holding has successfully captured the spirit of enterprise which resulted in the development of the various undertakings. He traces the amalgamations and changes to the present time, and future developments proposed for the area indicate a firm commitment to bus operation for many years to come.

It is perhaps not generally realised these days that intense competition was normal practice between bus operators in the halcyon days just after the first world war, and while visible competition has long since disappeared, there is still a keen sense of rivalry among many of the remaining independent operators. Much flavour is added to the transport scene by the independents and they still provide many important facilities in this part of England.

Mr Holding is to be congratulated for undertaking so successfully the vast amount of research necessary to enable this history to be written. The period which he has covered will no doubt be remembered as the most interesting phase of all in the development of road passenger transport because of the personalities involved and the variety which ensued. Nevertheless I am sure that the story is by no means concluded and the development over the next few years, while perhaps not so colourful, will continue to demonstrate the ever changing face of transport.

I would commend this book, not only to those interested in transport history, but to anyone interested in the North-East scene, in that the style and presentation enable one to appreciate some of the varying characteristics of the region and its people.

G. E. Hutchinson, MCIT
Director of Integrated Operations,
Tyne & Wear Passenger Transport Executive

INTRODUCTION

This book brings together for the first time the history of the bus and coach business in the North-Eastern corner of England. As one might expect in a territory which is nearly 200 miles from one end (Berwick) to the other (Spurn Head), it is enormously varied in character, and it has been well endowed with entrepreneurs able to see the profits that were to be made. Only a dwindling number of pioneers survive, but in some cases their spirit can be found in younger men who ensure the industry's vigorous condition in the 1970s.

Three large 'territorial' companies – United, Northern General, and East Yorkshire – have increasingly come to dominate the area, which has been chosen to correspond to their territories. Until April 1974 a convenient boundary also existed in the administrative counties, involving Northumberland, Durham and the North and East Ridings; the creation of the new North Yorkshire and Humberside counties brings to an end this coincidence of company and local government boundaries, but a convenient natural southern border exists in the rivers Ure, Ouse and Humber.

The native of this area suspects that the southerner regards it as 'a community that baths in zinc tubs in front of coal fires and thinks of little else than beer, bingo, and wife-baiting', as *The Times* once put it. We shall not presume such a degree of ignorance, but even so it may do no harm to dwell a little on the geographical contrasts and socio-economic background of the region. It can hardly be said to have a character since there are enormous variations, from densely populated industrial areas to inaccessible moorland; they may be found within surprisingly short distances of each other and, naturally, affect the public transport that has been found necessary and profitable over the years. For example, the main road (A696) north-west from Newcastle to Jedburgh justifies no more than half-a-dozen buses daily beyond Ponteland, six miles from the city centre – and these have changed hands several times over the years.

As we shall see, the Great North Road (A1) can often be recognised as the dividing line between natural economic regions, and this is nowhere more true than in Northumberland. The coalfield is, and always has been, almost exclusively to the east of the road, with the exception of the Tyne valley, where there are outcrops upstream of Hexham; northwards, apart from isolated collieries around Amble, it comes to an end near Ashington. Thus to the north the narrow coastal strip is agricultural except where tourism has been encouraged by excellent beaches and a series of medieval castles. The major companies have annexed only the area east of the A1 and the Tyne valley, the remainder being the problem area of the county. The Rural Community Council reported: 'Mid-Northumberland is an area containing extensive tracts of upland, limited physical resources, a small and scattered population and a rural economy based on farming.' Reorganisation in 1974 transferred to the new Tyne & Wear County only a quarter of the acreage, but half the population and rateable value, which could hardly help, and the area has suffered a rate of depopulation higher than that of the Scottish highlands and islands. Despite a county policy of concentrating industry and facilities in chosen market towns and 'growth points' and, later, of subsidising bus services to bring workers into these towns, it was found in 1971 that the decline had become more marked.

Again, in Durham the Great North Road can be seen as dividing the area of decline from that of growth and, to a lesser extent, the rural from the industrial. Collieries existed, of course, around the banks of the lower Tyne and Wear from very early times, but it was only with the development of railways and, later, the discovery of excellent coking coal in the west that large-scale exploitation began. In 1871 Stanley was characterised as 'a hamlet in the north of Durham, $4\frac{1}{2}$ miles north-north-east of Lanchester'; by 1901 the town had a population of 13,500. In many cases totally new communities appeared around the pithead, often on exposed hillsides and intended to be self-contained.

Like all good things the coal boom came to an end, but West Durham suffered particularly by its dependence on the one industry. Between 1920 and 1950 85 collieries west of Bishop Auckland, and 23 west of Crook were closed, and by 1970 there were none in either area. Currently in the county there are 31 working collieries, of which only nine lie west of the A1 – indeed the active collieries are so concentrated in the east that eight of those remaining, constituting all the 'long-life' pits, are sited on the coast and involve workings under the North Sea.

The effect of this on the social and industrial pattern, and thus on transport, cannot be overestimated. The 7,500 colliery redundances between 1948 and 1969 called for an extensive programme of employment creation and new housing away from the older mining villages (the main raison d'être of the Peterlee and Washington New Towns). However, the Coal Board successfully pursued a policy of transferring miners to other collieries in preference to redundancy, thus creating a transport demand, generally from west to east, of which firms such as Northern and Venture quickly took advantage. Meanwhile, Durham County Council acquired notoriety in planning circles by its institution in 1954 of a policy which divided communities into four categories; in the fourth category (D), which were ex-mining villages, no development of any kind was to be permitted, with a view to these settlements eventually being abandoned. Whereas one might have expected public transport to these villages to have declined as did the communities and their industry, apart from particular areas (notably Tow Law) this was not so; the need for transport to more distant employment kept services going and the pit villages continued to be relatively good bus country, as they have always been.

But Durham is not all mining. No collieries are to be found south of a line linking Shildon, Sedgefield and Hartlepool and here, with the exception of the industrial town of Darlington, all is agricultural. At any rate, this is true inland, for at the mouth of the Tees is the industrial success story of the North East. The ball started rolling with the export of Durham coal through Stockton by Stephenson's railway. Until 1850 the south bank of the Tees, from Stockton to Redcar, lacked serviceable roads and was regarded simply as pastureland for horses, but in that year iron was found in the Cleveland Hills to the south, hence the steelworks of Middlesbrough, 'the very prototype of a town born and reared in the past century'. It was the boom town of the 1870s, and if there is anywhere in the North East which corresponds nowadays to the southern caricature of industry, dirt and decay, it is the eastern outskirts of Middlesbrough. Cleveland iron ore is now worked out, leaving a wake of mining villages with as little future as those in Durham's category D, but the steelworks remain (and have recently expanded); in the first part of this century the foundations were laid for ICI's huge chemical plants at Billingham and Wilton; finally came petroleum refineries. Today the principal employer is still the steel industry, with chemicals and petroleum second and engineering/shipbuilding (using local steel) third. Much of what is true of the area commonly called Teesside is also true of Hartlepool to the north, with its own docks and steelworks, but Hartlepool has not enjoyed an influx of new industry to the same extent. As one might expect, the economic links between the two are growing and the coastal strip between is becoming industrialised, but much of the communication is in the form of Hartlepool people commuting to Billingham and Stockton.

Most of Durham breaks the rule that major lines of communication usually follow river valleys, for the flattish plateau makes for easier movement than the rivers, which cut their way through the upland – often meandering in deep defiles or denes. It is only in the extreme west that the hills become too rugged, where a series of rivers flowing eastwards from the Pennines provide the easiest route. These are the Dales, continuing south into North Yorkshire, and all but one taking their names from the rivers which flow down them – Wear, Tees, Swale, Ure (Wensleydale) and, outside our territory, the Nidd and Wharfe. Nowadays the Dales are overwhelmingly agricultural, but all except Wensleydale once had important lead-mining industries. Cheaper sources of lead from abroad brought about their decline at the turn of the century, and all that the casual traveller will notice now are unnaturally-shaped hills and the occasional chimney. Lead has given way to limestone, cement and gravel extraction in some cases, – notably in Weardale, where traffic is sufficient to have kept the railway line open 20 years after passenger services ceased. Only Wensleydale has no history of mining, its industry being the cheese for which it is well known. Originally this was made from surplus ewe's milk which could not then be transported to the larger towns at the bottom of the dale, and apart from cheese the main activity continues to be sheep-farming. As in Northumberland, there is a depopulation problem in the Dales, of the order of 13 per cent in the 20 years to 1971, and given the remoteness of the area one might suppose public transport to be poor; in fact most of the valleys enjoy good bus services, while there is little need or provision for communication across the watersheds.

The Great North Road marks a transition once more in North Yorkshire. To the east the Dales give way to the Cleveland Hills and North Yorkshire Moors, an extensive area of upland broken by occasional valleys and roads, and to the Plain of York. It is said that ten per cent of all the fatstock in the UK is reared in the three Ridings of Yorkshire, much of which comes from the hill farms of the north and west; by comparison the Plain, and the Wolds stretching to the east, are prosperous mixed farming land.

The Wolds, occupying the bulk of the East Riding between Hull, Malton and Filey, provide relief from the Plain, but, never rising as high as 1000ft, do little to discourage the prosperity of their market centres at Driffield, Pocklington and Market Weighton. With a longer history of wealth, it is no coincidence that some of Yorkshire's prettiest villages and best medieval churches are to be found here. It is significant too that one of the roles of the Plain and Wolds is that of provider of bloodstock and racecourses to the sporting public of the cities; Thirsk, York, Wetherby, Ripon and Beverley courses all fall within the area.

While land of this kind brings a steady income for its inhabitants, it has little to offer the bus operator. These parts of north and east Yorkshire have few large centres of population and such demand as exists is scattered. Fortunately, however, it has one considerable asset in its coastline, which has been developed to cater for city holidaymakers; carrying them to and around the resorts has helped to keep rural buses going, and many villages are directly served by routes which double as links between city and coast (Leeds – York – Scarborough, Leeds – York – Bridlington, Hull – Bridlington – Scarborough).

The resorts stretch at intervals from Redcar, within sight of the Teesside steelworks, almost to the Humber at Withernsea, and vary from the brash commercialism of the former to the quiet of the latter. The centre of gravity is undoubtedly midway between, where in close proximity are Scarborough, Filey and Bridlington, three fishing towns which developed in different ways. First Scarborough, blessed with mineral waters, attracted the gentility in the 18th century – and retains its quiet North Bay to contrast with the beer-and-cockles South; Bridlington

11

grew purely as a mass-appeal resort, and Filey was chosen for a huge holiday camp. A serious problem of coastal erosion exists southwards from Bridlington to Spurn Head, where once a town existed which returned a member to Parliament – and now the lifeboat station is regarded as so remote that it is the only one in the country staffed by a full-time crew. This south-eastern corner of Yorkshire (Holderness) is eroding at the rate of 7ft a year.

Finally we come to the natural southern boundary of the county. The Humber was a natural site for ports which exported Yorkshire and Midlands produce and imported the goods, including fish, needed by a growing population. While retaining some industry, small ports such as Goole and Selby have had over the centuries to recognise the natural advantages of Kingston-upon-Hull, nearer the North Sea. Thus Hull, already recognised as a port in the thirteenth century, grew to become the country's third largest by cargo value. Since the principal goods handled are fish, grain and timber, this indicates a very considerable traffic, but with containerisation, poor road access and a reputation for unhappy industrial relations, some has been lost to younger competing ports. There is a danger, therefore, of Hull's relative remoteness and association with one industry leading to a repetition of past employment problems in the North East, although connection to the motorway network, and the Humber bridge, may stabilise matters. Indeed, from being industrially the preserve of a few companies (Reckitt and Colman at Hull, Armstrong's at Beverley) Humberside could become the growth area of the 1980s.

We must now briefly examine the bus industry in the area as a whole. The counties concerned have among the lowest car ownership figures in the country, a situation which undoubtedly arises from the generally low level of employment and income. However, from the Cleveland Hills northwards as far as the Northumberland coalfield there is also a dense population. Of the enormous number of operators once in business, many survive, and they have not lost as high a proportion of their passengers in recent years as those in other parts. One speculates whether frequent services, partly the result of competition, have themselves helped to slow down the advance of the car.

We have seen that the changing industrial pattern, not least the closure of collieries, has increased the demand for specialised workers' transport. In an area where most people still travel to work by bus this has brought considerable opportunities to the operators. The extreme example is the office of the Department of Health & Social Security which was brought to Longbenton, just to the North-east of Newcastle by Government regional policies in late 1946, and employs about 11,000 people. A total of 60 special buses run daily to the complex, operated by the Northern Group (24), United (23) and the Passenger Transport Executive (13), and carrying about 3500 passengers — quite apart from those travelling by regular PTE and railway services. The new towns, large industrial estates at Team Valley and Spennymoor, and smaller estates all over the region, present examples of similar operations. In making these arrangements, many of those involved were helped by their experience of providing similar services for workers in the older heavy industries — steelworks at Consett, on Teesside, and the shipyards and engineering works of Tyneside — which had always been important.

Ideally history should begin at the beginning and continue until it reaches the end. However, while a historical sequence is desirable, in this book we are dealing with a very large and varied area and an abnormally large number of operators; Bishop Auckland in particular has always been notable for the spectrum of colours to be seen on its buses. In the preparation of this book I decided generally to treat each firm separately, although where independents are territorially close they have been grouped together, and because of the common ground between many express coach businesses, they have been given a separate chapter. Again, the very many businesses that have been absorbed usually appear under the organisation which ultimately ran their services.

My main regret is that in endeavouring to cover such an area it has been necessary to omit much fascinating detail. Given the considerable material to be found, and the very willing assistance given to me by nearly all the operators — and others — there is an ideal opportunity for someone with plenty of enthusiasm and time to produce an individual work on almost any of them!

D.H.

1

UNITED AUTOMOBILE SERVICES

The Early Days: Consolidation

The company was registerd on 4 April 1912 by its founder and first general manager, E. B. Hutchinson, under the same name as today but at Lowestoft in Suffolk. Before the year-end, however, a depot had been opened at Bishop Auckland to run a service thence to Durham, and began the development of one of the company's busiest operating areas of today. Growth before the outbreak of the first world war was confined to the takeover of the Great Eastern Railway's road services in East Anglia (Hutchinson had been a railwayman and this was one of the purposes behind the company's creation) but once hostilities were over the ambition of creating a territorial monopoly covering the whole of the east coast was keenly pursued.

The traffic potential of the densely populated Durham and Northumberland coalfields was obviously greater than that of Suffolk, and, despite growing competition, expansion was concentrated in these areas; depots were opened in Blyth and Ashington in 1919 and in Stockton in 1920, while also in 1919 a factory was opened in Lowestoft to build bus bodies, principally on ex-military goods chassis, since new buses were difficult to obtain. Later, these premises passed to the Eastern Counties Omnibus Co and were subsequently renamed Eastern Coach Works.

The downturn in industrial activity which followed the post-war boom soon acquired the far more serious character of a depression which was to affect the North East as much as any part of the country. For the only time in the company's history, no dividend was paid to investors in 1922, but this did not prevent expansion, a depot being opened in Ripon during the year – a very different proposition, being a prosperous market town surrounded by a purely agricultural area. One of the more interesting, and remarkably modern, marketing devices used to

15

attract passengers from competitors was the Kodak gift scheme, described in the staff magazine:

> The Kodak company photographed a number of interesting castles, churches, country houses, etc, in the areas served by United, and these views were printed in miniature on cards similar in size to the then popular cigarette cards. On the back of each card was a description of the buildings and it was stated briefly how one could get there by a United service or excursion. Each conductor was given a supply of cards, which were in sets numbered 1–25, and every passenger who purchased a return ticket of not less than one shilling, was presented with a card. Any person presenting a full set at District Office was given a free Kodak camera. Needless to say, it was not easy to collect a full set.

Naturally, United was not alone in the use of these promotional techniques and some operators, again anticipating present trends in fare collection, sold tickets to shopkeepers at a discount, so avoiding the handling of cash on buses; in one case tickets were given away with groceries like trading stamps.

Territorially, United's main aim in the early post-war years was to close the gap between its entirely separate businesses in East Anglia and the North East. It concentrated on Lincolnshire, where a number of subsidiaries were set up, and Nottinghamshire, where an interest was obtained in the Clowne-based firm of W. T. Underwood in 1923. Four years later, after another local business had been purchased, the two were formed into a new company, East Midland Motor Services Ltd, of which E. B. Hutchinson was chairman. At the same time the tentacles of the business began to stretch from Teesside down the Yorkshire coast towards Scarborough, where another isolated outpost was set up.

So far, United's growth had been purely internal. The absence of an effective licensing system, meaning free entry to the market, prevented the guarantee of a monopoly, but it was clear that financial success could in many cases only be assured by the purchase of competing businesses. At the same time, United was far from being the only ambitious operator, and other companies, together with the trams and sometimes motor buses of the municipalities, were seeking to carry passengers in many of the same places. It seemed sensible, therefore, to make what became known as area agreements with the companies (see John Hibbs, *The History of British Bus Services*, pp. 71–3), defining operating territories, whereas local authorities could effectively prevent any competition with their own fleets, if they so chose, by use of existing licensing powers. Within a few years the whole country was parcelled out between the companies, even though in some cases their buses never served every part of the area and there were, of course, thousands of smaller businesses which were not party to the agreements.

Probably the most formidable of United's competitors among the companies was Northern General (chapter 2), whose territory had spread southwards towards United's Durham area from its origin as an offshoot of the British Electric Traction group's trams on Tyneside; also under the Northern umbrella was the Tynemouth subsidiary whose buses in South Northumberland were on United's doorstep. (A UAS depot had been opened in Newcastle by 1922 to serve this area.) The agreement made with Northern in 1924 allocated to United the area south of a line passing from west to east through Durham and Easington village, Northern running north of this line. This border was adhered to fairly rigidly until recently. Although the Tyne might have seemed an obvious northern boundary between the companies, BET control over the Tynemouth company on the north bank prevented this, and the line was drawn from Whitley Bay west-south-west to Newcastle; west of the city it corresponded with the County Durham border, so that those parts of Northumberland south of the Tyne were (and are) served by United, in so far as large-company buses cover this generally rural area at all.

This agreement has had the curious and unique effect of dividing United's operations into two self-contained territories between which ran the rival Northern company. (The same could be said of other parts of the country at the time, but none has proved so long-lasting.) The division is enhanced by the fact that United busmen in Northumberland are members of the National Union of Railwaymen, but those south of the Tyne of the Transport & General Workers Union; moreover the company gives greater autonomy to the Northumberland area than the others, recognising both its physical distance from headquarters and that its fleet of 365 buses is equal to that of many autonomous companies.

17

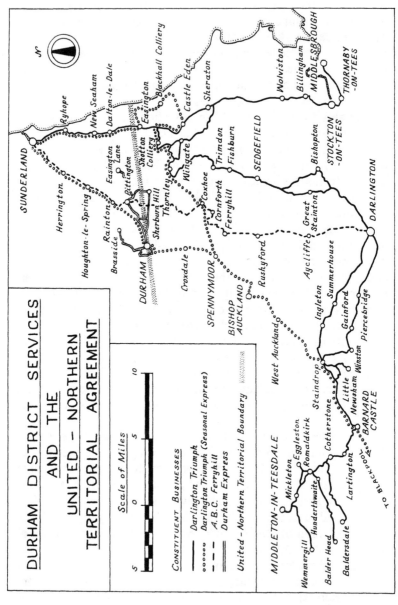

DURHAM DISTRICT SERVICES
AND THE
UNITED — NORTHERN
TERRITORIAL AGREEMENT

Scale of Miles

CONSTITUENT BUSINESSES

——— Darlington Triumph
ooooooo Darlington Triumph (Seasonal Express)
— — — A.B.C. Ferryhill
Durham Express

United — Northern Territorial Boundary

Fig. 1

It was clearly undesirable that an agreement should lead to unnatural route patterns, and a through running agreement was made between the companies, leading to jointly-run services across the Durham and Easington 'frontiers', and so to United buses running into Newcastle from Co Durham (see Fig. 1), but they have never been operated by Northumberland-based buses. They have shown quite remarkable continuity, using the same basic route numbers, frequency and timetables for over 40 years! Nor did through running necessarily mean through fares. Much of the nature of the United/Northern relationship over the years is summed up in the fact that they could not agree on a system for dividing revenue from the joint routes, and so passengers were required to re-book on crossing the border at Durham or Easington, except, curiously, on the Newcastle–Bishop Auckland route, where through fares on the competing OK service obliged them to offer the same. This anachronism was not removed until 1971, and to this day there is no form of multi-journey ticket available for any journey across the frontier, a fact which greatly incensed the author when commuting between Peterlee and Newcastle in 1970/71.

Under New Management

Thus by 1926 United's territory was fairly clearly defined, although in many parts its coverage was thin. E. B. Hutchinson therefore set about the acquisition of small businesses in much greater numbers, and in doing so established a network, much of which has survived to the present day.

Between 1923 and 1926 the fleet nearly doubled; businesses acquired over the next four years included Robinson's Motors of Scarborough (1926), giving services in the Whitby area which filled the gap between the existing Teesside and Scarborough operations, and Amos Proud (1928) who ran 45 buses based in South Northumberland, but with outstations at Alnwick, Berwick, Dunbar and Edinburgh. From this firm came not only routes and buses, but future management in Charles Dickinson, who moved to United and became traffic manager, retiring in 1971. It is not surprising that a man of such long service should become known for his very detailed knowledge of the company's history and operations. In view of the concentration of expansion in the North East, the decision was taken to move the head office from Lowestoft to a more central position at York, although the company had very little operation in the immediate area. Fleet standardisation and improvement became increasingly important, and the company received 140 new buses in 1927, 125 in 1928 and about 150 in 1929.

However, although United was big by contemporary standards, it was far from being the biggest bus organisation, and its dynamic growth was itself bound to attract attention. Moreover, other bus businesses were not the only buyers in the market, for the railway companies, grouped since 1923 into the 'big four', were showing an increasing interest in bus control. The former North Eastern Railway had been a pioneer in bus operation itself, much of its activity being in United's territory, and predating the existence of the company. As early as 1904 a service was introduced to link Ripon station with the town, extended to Studley Royal (Fountains Abbey) during the summer. This led to a sizeable business in day tours based on the holiday towns of Bridlington (1905), Scarborough (1906), Harrogate (1907) and Whitby (1912). Charabancs of foreign manufacture were used, many having interchangeable bodies so that they could be used to carry freight in winter. Competition was stiff, and the early open-sided charabancs were, by 1912, considered inferior to the modern 'torpedo' styled bodies and 19 were rebodied in this style by the NER itself by the outbreak of world war I. These tours were suspended during the war and not recommenced; after 1923 the LNER disposed of the Scarborough business to Robinson's Motors, which was subsequently purchased by United. The company's tours from Scarborough still run from the station forecourt.

In 1905 the NER obtained an Act of Parliament which, inter alia, permitted the company to provide omnibuses and carry mail, the cue for the introduction of more regular routes. Among the first were a Thirsk station service (1906), and one from Blyth to Hartford (1907), but most important was a concentration of routes in the Durham area which grew up from 1912. All were intended to connect mining villages with a railhead where there was no direct rail facility, to encourage through travel, but in the event most traffic was local with little transfer to the railway. Few routes of this kind were economic and, if the incentive of extra rail traffic was absent, it is not surprising that there was never a really comprehensive network.

20

After wartime suspension, the Durham routes were re-introduced, and expanded in 1922, despite losses from 1921 onwards, which undoubtedly arose from competition. Losses in 1927 amounted to £4,792 from 20 buses, which makes it all the more surprising that in 1928 a fleet of new Thorneycrofts was purchased. However, by this time fierce competition among road operators was affecting not only themselves but also rail traffic. The railway companies came to the view that to protect themselves they should invest heavily in buses, but that it would be foolish to add their vehicles to the already vicious competition. Thus they set about purchasing established businesses, aided by Railway (Road Traffic) Acts which became law on 3 August 1928 and gave the companies general road powers; some, including the NER, had anticipated legislation by obtaining powers themselves, or operating without them.

At this stage we must turn to the other major bus groups. The British Electric Traction group, which had expanded from tramway beginnings to control such companies as Northern, has already been referred to, but Thomas Tilling, originally London jobmaster and bus proprietor, was also by now deeply involved in provincial bus operation. BET had formed a subsidiary, British Automobile Traction, to look after its buses, and after some joint ventures by BAT and Tilling, the latter acquired an interest in BAT in 1922, and nominated two directors. Thus by 1928 BAT was interested in 19 companies, in 11 of which Tillings also had a share, and BAT itself was partly Tilling-owned. To simplify this situation a new holding company, Tilling & BAT Ltd, was formed, with a stronger Tilling interest, to own the individual BAT companies. However, not all BET companies went into the pool, those with strong tramway interests (such as Northern) being excluded, though there was nothing to stop either group making fresh purchases independently.

After the passing of the Railway (Road Traffic) Acts, Tilling & BAT started negotiations with the railways. The latter were interested in acquiring bus operators both within and outside the combines, and the aim of Tilling & BAT was to tolerate not more than 50 per cent railway control, to prevent the emergence of a new, powerful, railway-owned group; the prolongation of discussions by the railways led Tilling & BAT to think that such

21

was indeed their purpose. When the large National and Crosville companies were bought by the railways early in 1929, J. F. Heaton, the dynamic vice-chairman of Tilling, was concerned that railway control of United as well would make too substantial a group for comfort, and on confirmation that the LNER had made an offer for United, he made a counter-bid,

IMPORTANT NOTICE!

REDUCTION OF FARES

JOHN LEE & SON,
ROTHBURY.

BEG TO ANNOUNCE TO THE TRAVELLING PUPLIC THAT THE FOLLOWING RATES BECOME EFFECTIVE ON AND AFTER

JUNE 8TH, 1925,
ON THEIR MOTOR SALOON SERVICES BETWEEN ROTHBURY AND NEWCASTLE.

		RETURN	SINGLE
THROPTON-NEWOASTLE		7/6	4/6
ROTHBURY	,,	6/-	4/-
BRINKBURN	,,	5/6	3/6
LONGFRAMLINGTON	,,	5/6	3/6
LONGHORSLEY	,,	4/6	3/-
ESPLEY	,,	4/-	2/6
MORPETH	,,	2/6	1/6

TIMES OF SERVICES
every week day, excepting Good Friday and Christmas Day

OUTWARDS.		RETURN.	
Thropton	8- 0 a.m.	Newcastle -	6 p.m.
Rothbury	8-15 ,,	(Haymarket)	
Longframlington	8-30 ,,		
Longhorsley	8-45 ,,		

→ EXTRA SERVICE ON MONDAYS AND SATURDAYS ONLY. ←

Leave NEWCASTLE for ROTHBURY	-	-	10-30 a.m.
Leave ROTHBURY for NEWCASTLE	-	-	3-45 p.m.

TRAVEL BY THE LUXURIOUS SALOONS USED IN ABOVE SERVICES, ON THE KINGS HIGHWAYS, AND ENJOY YOUR HOLIDAY :: :: ::

Smith & Company, Printers, Rothbury.

Fig. 2

subject to confirmation by the Tilling & BAT board. There was some argument with the BET group of directors on whether they would support the bid, but when it became clear that Tilling would otherwise go it alone, they agreed to support Heaton, and United shareholders were recommended to accept the Tilling & BAT offer. At this stage Heaton offered to resell 50 per cent of the shares to the LNER at net cost, in order to avoid competitive bidding for control. This did not immediately succeed, but finally agreement was made on a joint offer to United shareholders, with the effect that the bulk of United shareholding was divided equally between the LNER and Tilling & BAT, a small proportion remaining in private hands. E. B. Hutchinson had determined that, whichever party was to control United, he would not stay at the helm, and he duly resigned. He was succeeded as general manager by H. P. Stokes, who came from Plymouth Corporation, and was perhaps most notable for being the father of Lord Stokes, the future chairman of British Leyland.

Hutchinson has been rightly called a character, but not in the extrovert sense. He was in fact very quiet and astute; knowledgeable despite his lack of the professional qualifications held by his successors, he would listen in silence to an argument proceeding, then demolish it in half a dozen words. The spread of United interests across the country shows him to be an exponent of the early busman's art of building up business from scratch in various centres.

To mark the change of ownership United's colour scheme changed. At one time grey, buses had during the 1920s been painted bright yellow; now they changed to the red and cream which was one of two standard Tilling liveries. Another 40 years passed before the distinctive style of fleetname

$$\underline{U}^{NITED}$$

fell out of use.

The 1930s : Development Under Regulation

The new regime under Tilling & BAT/railway control had the most profound effect on United's operating area. The LNER had bought businesses in areas outside the North East where

United was running, and the decision was taken to form new companies to absorb these various interests; thus the Eastern Counties Omnibus and Lincolnshire Road Car companies were created and, as a result of United's concentration in the North East, the headquarters were again moved in 1932 to the present premises in Darlington. United was partially compensated for the loss by the transfer to it of the LNER's own road services within its territory (mainly around Durham), together with smaller businesses which the LNER had bought in 1929, including quite small firms, such as Billingham and Haverton Hill Motor Services.

Of far greater potential importance was the passing of the Road Traffic Act in 1930. The requirement that a bus should hold a public service vehicle licence, involving a mechanical inspection before a certificate of fitness could be granted, could not be attained by many small operators, who chose to sell their businesses; some feared that if they did not, the wealthy railways with their new powers would force them out. Others were not prepared to comply with the new system of road service licensing, which demanded that they run at regular times and at stable fares. Moreover, the incentive to large operators to buy out their small competitors was much greater, since although before 1930 there was no restriction on entry to a route, the new legislation favoured the established firm and so tended to create local monopolies; once a competitor was removed, he was removed for good. Finally, the injection of large amounts of railway capital provided funds to purchase the businesses of willing sellers, and United entered its greatest period of expansion.

Between 1921 and 1939, 129 businesses were bought at a total cost of £1,075,709. The fleet was initially reduced in size by transfers to the new companies, but afterwards steadily rose, from 618 buses in 1932 to 850 in 1938. Some of the coach businesses acquired will be dealt with separately in chapter 4, and for the sake of brevity the other more important purchases are shown in tabular form:

Name	Base	Date of Acquisition	Services Operated	Remarks
J. Smith Safeway	Middlesbrough	1930	Middlesbrough–Newcastle Middlesbrough local Middlesbrough–Glasgow	
County MS	Northumberland	1933	London–Glasgow Whitley Bay–Glasgow	Succeeded Gordon & Sons, Choppington and taken over jointly with SMT. Whitley Bay service still operates – a popular holiday centre for Glaswegians
Thos. Allen	Blyth	1933	Newcastle–Ashington Newcastle–Aberdeen Blyth–Morpeth	
Ennis & Reed	Crook	1933	Newcastle–Crook	Purchased jointly with Northern
Rutherford		1932	Alnwick–Berwick	
John Lee	Rothbury	1928	Thropton–Newcastle	
Walters & Johnson	Ferryhill	1932	Durham–Darlington	
Northallerton Omnibus Services	Northallerton	1930	Northallerton–Wensleydale	
Eastern Express	West Hartlepool	1931	Hartlepool–Durham Hartlepool–Sunderland Hartlepool–Newcastle Stockton–Whitby	Purchased by LNER 1929 Ex Cleveland Bus Service 1929

In 1931 United buses replaced a Corporation tram fleet in Scarborough on terms which involved the separation of the town and country fleets, and a minimum fare on country routes within the borough. In the same year United and others replaced trams in Carlisle by buses which led the way to the development of rural services in the area east of Carlisle. In Darlington, Hartlepool, Middlesbrough and Stockton, United agreed to protect the Corporations by charging fares slightly in excess of those applying on municipal buses, but in Newcastle the situation was slightly different in that the Corporation ran services well outside the borough boundary into United territory. Here a series of agreements was made in the mid-1930s, whereby longer routes running outside the city to Cramlington, Branch End and Seaton Sluice were handed to United, in exchange for a Corporation monopoly to Darras Hall, a growing executive garden village north-west of the city.

By this time United had a large proportion of its services in the very rural areas of Northumberland and the North Riding, with a number of small depots and outstations. A good example is Hawes, the market town and cheese capital at the head of Wensleydale, with two buses based 28 miles from the nearest depot at Richmond to keep down empty running from town depots a good distance away. Bus travel in such areas has always been a more personal thing than in towns and cities, partly because the smaller establishment leads to valuable familiarity between staff and passengers.

Supervision here is in the hands of a resident inspector who remembers the days when:

> Baskets of eggs, rabbits, chickens and ducks were conveyed on the roof of the bus if a roof rack was fitted, but failing a roof rack they had to be carried inside the saloon with all the smell you can imagine on a hot day. Regular market-day travellers held their own personal seat on the bus and anyone taking the liberty of sitting there would be told it was Mrs So & So's seat. As the bus proceeded along the route everyone kept a look-out for the regulars and a shout would halt the driver if someone was struggling across the fields with a basket of eggs. On one occasion at Leyburn market the bus, a 14-seater Chevrolet with a standing load, was ready to depart when a local dealer asked if he could take a calf on board. The driver agreed if he would hurry up and get it, but he

changed his mind when he saw the dealer coming with a well grown animal led with a halter.

The United bus in the Yorkshire and Durham Dales, and in remoter Northumberland, still gives a very personal service.

The 1930s was undoubtedly the period of greatest growth in the bus industry generally, and United, benefiting like others from its privileged position under the licensing system, invested heavily in new premises and vehicles. In 1934 Stokes was succeeded as general manager by A. T. Evans, an accountant, like B. T. Pratt who in turn replaced Evans in 1959; it is probably not unfair to say that while financial control of United was (and is) very efficient, traffic and commercial developments during the subsequent period were of secondary importance. A. T. Evans was very close to Hutchinson, having been accountant in the East Anglian area, and he naturally followed his policies. He was secretary and traffic manager until he became general manager, a post he held exactly 25 years. B. T. Pratt, similarly, had been secretary first. Consequently policies were decided for 40 years very much from a financial point of view.

The second world war affected United in much the same way as other operators; there were problems of staff, vehicle and fuel shortages, conversions to producer-gas operation, and demands for the carriage of such special traffic as troops, munition workers and evacuees; long-distance and seasonal services were suspended. An event which was to be of great importance later occurred in 1942 when the uneasy alliance between the Tilling and BET groups came to an end; the companies were divided between the partners, generally, but not always, on a basis of original ownership. United passed to Tilling, so widening the gap between the United company and the BET-owned Northern group.

Post-War: Newer Management, New Problems

The Transport Act, 1947, brought about the nationalisation of the four main-line railway companies and their subsidiaries, in-land waterways, most road haulage, and London Transport, but not, directly, that of road passenger transport. However, the railway shares in bus companies that had been acquired in 1929/30, often amounting to 49 per cent, came into State hands on 1 January 1948. More significantly, the Act provided for the development of area schemes for the co-ordination of road passenger transport, which would clearly involve the compulsory purchase of businesses involved. Thinking that ultimate nationalisation was inevitable, the Tilling Group decided to sell its interests to the State, and so United came completely under the control of a grateful British Transport Commission on 1 September 1948.

The two pilot areas chosen for area schemes were East Anglia and Northumberland/Durham – both with many independently-owned fleets. As Hibbs has commented, the Act 'did not make it clear whether all undertakings ... were to be acquired or not' but those involved in the North-East scheme included 8 municipal fleets, 3 firms with over 100 vehicles, 6 with between 25 and 99, and 197 with under 25, not apparently chosen purely according to the amount of stage carriage work performed. At a public inquiry held in 1951 the municipalities, particularly Newcastle, expressed strong objection to the loss of control of their local fleets, and in any event the election of a Conservative Government later in the same year removed any likelihood of compulsory nationalisation.

Meanwhile the BTC, which strongly favoured the scheme as a way of building its own empire, was in 1949 offering generous terms to independents willing to sell, and in both areas some, aware of the advancing age of their vehicles and of a slight decline in traffic, seized the opportunity. A problem arose in that all three businesses in Co Durham which decided to sell, operated across the United/Northern territorial boundary (see Fig. 1) and the BTC could not take the obvious step of attaching the services to United without infringing an agreement with a BET company. A solution was found in the creation of a new operator, Durham District Services, to take over these businesses, legally separate from United but with a common headquarters and the same management personnel; its buses were painted Tilling green in contrast to the Tilling red of United. We may best consider the DDS constituents separately.

Darlington Triumph Services Ltd (D. T. Todd) This business was established in the mid 1920s with depots at Darlington, Sunderland and Barnard Castle. Its lengthy routes connected Sunderland with Middlesbrough, Darlington, Barnard Castle and Blackpool and Darlington with Barnard Castle, while a subsidiary, the Fawn Lea Omnibus Co, ran from Barnard Castle into Upper Teesdale. It ran a mixed and mostly aged fleet of over 50 buses, of which five were double-deck.

ABC Services Ferryhill The ABC represented Aaron Brothers, E. & R. Binks, and P. J. Coulson & Son, who had originally been partners in another route from Darlington to Sunderland via Ferryhill. Established in 1928, it also had an assorted selection of 20 single-deck vehicles; in 1946 Coulson sold his share of the business to Aaron Bros.

Express Omnibus Co (Durham) Ltd Also founded in 1928 and also running about 20 single-deck buses, Express operated Durham local services and from the city to Easington Lane and Sherburn Hill.

Thus Durham District Services commenced operations with about 90 very assorted vehicles. The older buses were quickly replaced by transfers from the main United fleet, and this became common practice, so that shortly before the absorption of DDS into United in 1969, of a 64-bus fleet 23 had been so transferred. The job of rationalising DDS was given to D. S. Deacon, then assistant traffic manager, who rose to become deputy general manager of United and, later, chairman of the southern region of the National Bus Company.

Over the country as a whole the post-war boom in bus traffic was ending, and giving way to a decline. United's peak in passenger numbers seems to have been reached in about 1954, and in that year the Bell's Services subsidiary, acquired in 1946, was passed to Armstrong of Westerhope (chapter 7). A more significant reaction was the introduction of one-man operation in 1956; initially this was on loss-making routes in Northumberland and Yorkshire, being extended later into Co Durham. Today one-man operation is the rule rather than the exception, around two-thirds of all operations being on this basis at the time of writing, and few or no double crews remain at the smaller depots.

The problem of declining traffic was as great for many independents as for major companies, particularly in rural areas, and, remembering that many were at this time feeling the need of a successor to a proprietor who had founded the business in the 1920s, it is not surprising that the remainder of this section deals with takeovers. One of the more sizeable, in 1957, was that from Scott's Greys of the business once owned by James and Mosley, running to Middleton-One-Row, Neasham and Cowton, while in

1965 Crowe Bros, who ran from Stockton to Stokesley and Swainby, ceased operation and left United to step into the breach. Two other acquisitions were of better-known firms whose histories are interesting illustrations of licensing law, and therefore merit more attention.

The business of Norfolk of New Ridley (in Northumberland, south of the Tyne) started in 1926 when N. W. Norfolk became a member of the Private Owners Association of Blaydon, which ran between Newcastle and Hexham along the South bank of the Tyne, now United route 601. The Association was later renamed the Blaydon and District Omnibus Proprietors Association and became a company in 1929, but Norfolk chose not to join. Soon after, he joined with five other operators known as the Tyne and Allen Co to run between Newcastle and Allendale via Hexham, but this lasted for only four months.

In 1931, by which time the Road Traffic Act was in force, Norfolk applied for a licence from Kilnpit Hill to Newcastle, which was granted subject to protective fares over the section from Stocksfield to Newcastle, so that the other operators running to Hexham should not lose traffic to Norfolk. After the second world war business boomed temporarily, especially since the route passed a favourite Tyneside beauty spot at Apperley Dene, but it was short-lived; the service to Kilnpit Hill was withdrawn and extended beyond Apperley Dene to Scales Cross on three days a week. The firm was clearly at a disadvantage in having to charge higher fares than others (now United and Venture) over the section of route where revenue potential was greatest; in 1957 Norfolk's application to have the protection removed was granted despite objections, on grounds of the great discrepancy between United and Venture's high frequency and the small-scale Norfolk operation, generally involving only one bus.

United took over the service from the blue and cream Norfolk fleet of Dennis Lancets in 1964, and the route continues much as before. It is interesting, however, that in 1972 some of the Scales Cross journeys were diverted to serve Hedley-on-the-Hill, the terminus of an abandoned Venture route.

Wilkinson's Motor Services of Sedgefield was founded in 1919, running from Stockton to Fishburn and from Trimdon Grange to Darlington. It continued until 1929, when, perhaps in anticipation of the Road Traffic Act, the Fishburn route was extended through Ferryhill to Spennymoor, and the other route was sold to Darlington Triumph (and thus passed to DDS in 1950, by which time it had been extended to Sunderland). At the same time Thomas Wilkinson started a pair of express services to Blackpool from the mining villages in East Durham, and apart from temporary wartime restrictions there was until 1963 no change in the pattern of routes.

In that year a new managing director, appointed in 1960 when the firm was made a limited company, applied to extend the Spennymoor route (ie the one stage carriage service) to Willington via Page Bank, which exactly duplicated a Page Bank service operated by J. Jewitt of Spennymoor. Not surprisingly Jewitt objected and applied to extend his route to Willington similarly, but the highway authority objected to both operators using the new stretch of road. Wilkinson's next move was to propose an alternative route to Willington via Binchester, which this time bore a close resemblance to the solitary Byers Green-Spennymoor route of Shaw Bros. There was again an objection and a proposal to extend Shaw Bros' route to Willington, but on this occasion Wilkinson was successful.

Soon after, further expansion came with the purchase from Scurrs Motor Services, Stillington, of a share in a route from Middlesbrough to Bishop Auckland, then run jointly by them with L. A. & E. G. Harwood, better known as Favourite Service No 2. This route was identical to Wilkinson's original Stockton-Spennymoor route with extensions at each end, and the two together gave a 30min frequency. The Middlesbrough-Stockton section of the acquired route was soon abandoned and this was the pattern existing when United took over in February 1967.

After acquisition the Willington route was further extended through Crook, but perhaps the most interesting development has been the entry on the scene of Wilkinson's neighbour and competitor, Trimdon Motor Services (chapter 7). Trimdon was known to be interested in the Wilkinson business (perhaps explaining United's sudden decision to purchase) and, having lost this opportunity, not only took over the remainder of Scurr's business but also that of Harwood. Indeed, Favourite was so incensed that the route which Scurr's had carefully sold to Wilkinson, to keep it out of United's clutches, had in fact fallen to United, that it made doubly sure of passing its share to the one firm it thought would never voluntarily sell. The obliged

United and Trimdon on this one route to acknowledge each other's existence, in contrast to other common sections of route.

The Present : Changes and Opportunities

In 1967 there was a further threat of widespread nationalisation, which, like that of 20 years earlier, had an indirect effect on United. In 1962 the British Transport Commission had been wound up and its road passenger interests transferred to the new Transport Holding Company, but this had no effect on the day-to-day affairs of the companies concerned. The sale in the late 1960s by BET of its British bus interests, including Northern, to the THC, dovetailed conveniently with Barbara Castle's Transport Act of 1968, and in 1969 the National Bus Company (NBC) was set up to control the combined bus operation; now that both old rivals were state-owned, territorial agreements ceased to have the same significance.

It should not be thought, however, that the agreements were unchangeable. In 1967, before the takeover, United entered a co-ordination scheme with BET-owned East Yorkshire involving the two companies' Scarborough-Bridlington routes and the closure of United's Bridlington outstation. On the other hand, apparently desirable territorial changes even within the Tilling Group were not easily achieved; in the same year it was proposed that the West Yorkshire company should hand over its operations at Scarborough in exchange for United's Ripon depot. United had a remarkable array of routes, many running only a few market journeys a week and generally very different in character from most of the route pattern, radiating from this most southerly depot. West Yorkshire's headquarters at Harrogate was only 11 miles away and connected by a frequent service, while Darlington was 33 miles distant and served directly only by the Tyne-Mersey service thrice daily. Ripon depot was almost self-contained operationally, and no major joint operation problems would arise, while there were regularly Ripon-based United buses waiting in Harrogate bus station which could be put to use; United's geographical area, fleet and rural services were much greater than West Yorkshire's, so that the change would balance matters somewhat. At the same time West Yorkshire's outpost of four buses at Scarborough was clearly too small to be economical, being by far the most distant from headquarters, and it was ready for complete one-man operation except for the problem of redundant conductors, who could be conveniently absorbed by United.

There were nevertheless arguments against the change, and in the end a compromise was reached whereby the bulk of United's idle buses in Harrogate were extended to Leeds, giving an improved through frequency from Ripon. The West Yorkshire bus station and depot in Scarborough were closed and operations transferred to United premises, the buses and drivers still being controlled by West Yorkshire while the conductors went to United. Since the coming of rural subsidies in 1971 (page 36) the Ripon services have been pruned considerably, one victim being a route to Pateley Bridge which, if West Yorkshire had taken over, could have been run far more efficiently by a bus already available at Pateley Bridge depot.

The first and most necessary of the changes brought about after the formation of the National Bus Company was the absorption of Durham District Services. Steps had already been taken to economise where possible, the separate depots at Durham and Darlington having been closed in 1961 and DDS buses being based at United depots in those towns and at Middlesbrough. Now there was no reason why United buses should not run north of the boundary, and the buses were thus painted red. In 1972 Ferryhill depot was closed and its work divided between Durham and Darlington, so that of the original depots only Barnard Castle and Sunderland now survive; indeed an attempt was made to transfer Sunderland work to Northern and the latter acquired licences for the purpose, but the DDS crews objected strongly to working for Northern. Undoubtedly this was partly because the corporate spirit and identity of a small team would be lost, but also they had far more one-man operation than Northern and did not wish to see the consequent bonus divided among all the Northern staff! Some DDS drivers said they would leave rather than transfer, even though they had been working out of the same depots for almost a decade. There is an apocryphal story of a DDS inspector who was asked by a passenger the times of buses to Bishop Auckland. 'Every two hours', said the inspector, 'and it's just gone'. As the passenger walked away he was told – 'But there's a United bus every 15 minutes.' What better epitaph for Durham District Services?

33

In the next territorial change United's boundaries were to shrink. In January 1969 Carlisle depot and the outstation at Alston were transferred to Ribble, an ex-BET company which ran the majority of town and country routes from Carlisle. Operations in this area, which were mostly rural but included a share in the Carlisle town routes, were self-contained (the backbone of the Pennines comes between them and the rest of United's area) to the extent that joint operation was necessary only on the long Carlisle-Newcastle route. It has been claimed that, in this case, high Ribble fares and staff difficulties in Carlisle led to a local desire for United to take over Ribble rather than vice-versa.

A small move towards an entente with Northern came in 1970. One of the original joint routes, No 55 from Newcastle to Middlesbrough, was cut back to Durham, in view of the excessive frequency between Durham and Newcastle, and became a United-only route. In order that a through facility should continue, Northern's limited-stop X1 between Newcastle and Durham was extended to Middlesbrough and became joint; United had already become involved in the limited-stop routes in 1966 when X5 from Newcastle to Hartlepool was introduced, but the important point here was that Northern buses running into Newcastle on X1 then worked the X2 to South Shields, and vice-versa, and this arrangement continued so that United ran jointly on a route which was clearly in Northern territory. As one might expect, there are many stories of Middlesbrough-based drivers, usually with an unfamiliar 'London' green-and-cream coach, getting lost in the Tyne Dock area while working this route. Over the next two years United took over sole control of Durham local routes, on which Northern previously had a major share on territorial grounds even though it did not have a depot in the city. Ownership of the bus station, basically unaltered in 40 years and hardly a credit to Northern, also changed hands. Rapprochement between the companies has continued, following the appointment of D. G. Rawlinson, United's general manager since 1969, as chief general manager for the North East, with a joint coaching organisation under a strictly neutral manager – but, significantly, administered from United premises at Gallowgate.

The new-born NBC faced its first major crisis in 1970, when the economics of bus operation, which had become

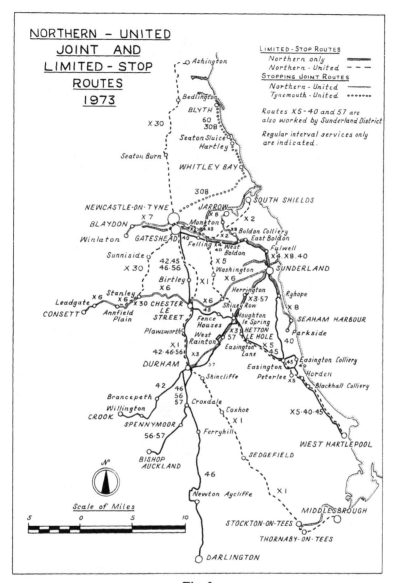

Fig. 3

progressively worse through the 1960s, deteriorated alarmingly, the principal ingredients being a decrease in passengers and available staff (leading to higher fares and lower reliability), and industrial action aimed at improving the relatively worsening pay of busmen. The 1968 Act which set up the NBC had also authorised local authorities to subsidise unremunerative rural services, in the now famous Section 34, but little action had been taken. After its subsidiaries had made general and ineffective pleas for help, NBC instructed them to prepare a list of unprofitable routes and to announce a date by which these would be withdrawn if subsidies were not forthcoming. In most counties, including the North Riding and Northumberland, this had the desired effect of opening the coffers, and in those areas comparatively few changes have been made to services. It is worth noting, however, that financial involvement has made the authorities look closely at exactly what services are needed, with the result that very poorly-used routes, such as some of those around Ripon, have gone, while elsewhere new subsidised routes have been introduced.

In contrast some counties, whether through dislike of NBC, political principle, or disbelief that the threat would be carried out, refused to pay, and could hardly have been surprised that bus routes were decimated. In Durham though a few ritual victims were sacrificed, mostly in the west of the county, no community of any size was deprived of a service. In one case a route was taken over by OK Motor Services (see p. 150), involving closure of Woodland outstation, and the direct Darlington-Sedgefield route was replaced by off-peak journeys from the villages to the town run on a marginal cost basis. Whether the survival of country buses in Durham without subsidy was due to better economics or, perhaps, to fear of the independents stepping in is uncertain, but it is fair to say that while Durham is by no means as rural as Northumberland or the North Riding, United's part of it in particular has its share of green fields.

In the same year (1971) another rural problem presented itself. The family business of Percival Bros, of Richmond, had been running buses to Barnard Castle and Swaledale since the early days, but one of the brothers had died, and upon the death of the second it was decided to dispose of the business. The services were of a 'deep rural' nature, to the extent that they could not normally qualify for exchequer assistance towards a local authority subsidy because revenue was less than half the cost of operation; however, the North Pennines Rural Development Board had seen fit to make up the deficiency. The

36

North Riding County Council advertised for operators to take over from Percival's, asking them to state what subsidy, if any, they would require, and the result was that United took over the main Swaledale route to Keld, while a feeder from Gunnerside to Arkengarthdale went to T. W. Harker. The Barnard Castle route passed initially to G. Maude but was later transferred to L. Burrell (Barnard Castle Coaches) who combined it with an existing service to Richmond. This was not quite the end of the story, for the incoming Conservative Government wound up the North Pennines Board and so removed the basis of the Swaledale finances, but since United was able to combine the route with others from Richmond depot the loss was reduced, so qualifying it for exchequer aid.

Conclusion

In recent years United has continued to be among the most successful financially of NBC companies; in the crisis year of 1970, when many companies showed losses, United's profit was little less than the total of all profitable companies. We may ask, therefore, why United enjoys this unusual success.

The answer must lie partly in the nature of its operating territory. The problems of bus operators in the 1960s could be summed up by saying that they either had plentiful staff and few passengers, or plentiful passengers and few staff, and United was one of the few fortunately placed in having enough of both. Staff turnover is distinctly low and staff relations have generally been good. It is noticeable also that the company has a high proportion of small country depots and outstations which, besides enjoying lower costs, also tend to offer a better community spirit than large urban units. *Motor Transport* observed in 1972 that the last bus from Hexham to the Allenheads outstation on Saturday night was timed to arrive at its terminus 8min after closing time, but that on this one journey nobody had ever complained about a regular habit of arriving about 15min early. One notices that the route in 1973 was accelerated to give a *scheduled* arrival before closing time.

Secondly the quality of management must have helped United's good record, for example, in industrial relations; in particular there has been a low turnover of general managers over the years (only six since 1912) and certainly there is evidence of a high standard of managerial enterprise in comparison with some NBC subsidiaries. Examples are the system of depot costing employed for many years before such a concept became common (and which may well have helped the retention of low-cost rural services), the company's printing press, which enables all its publicity material to be produced internally, and the close eye kept on new centres of employment and housing, (particularly trading estates and New Towns) so that services can be developed in accordance with, and often in advance of, changing demand. Particular routes that catch one's eye are to Holy Island, where the causeway can only be crossed at low water and so the timetable must vary according to the tides, and in the Berwick area, where the company prides itself on running into Scotland (apart from its joint routes with Eastern Scottish) and has in fact increased its operations since 1971 following withdrawal by the Scottish company.

Even so, United has not been able to escape the decline in bus travel. The total of passengers carried has steadily decreased and in accordance the fleet in recent years has dropped from 1,050 to 950 vehicles, part accounted for by the 1971 rural withdrawals but rather more by general rationalisation schemes, which in many cases have improved frequencies in growth areas while recognising a population loss in such areas as West Durham.

To balance a declining market, the company has vigorously pursued a growth policy in the coach and holiday sphere. In 1966 United became members of the Association of British Travel Agents, enabling 15 of its offices to handle a wide range of holiday business; its legal entanglements with Bee-Line Roadways, which will be referred to again in chapter 4, have brought some notoriety, and at the same time long-distance services, both established routes such as those to London and new ones, have increased their traffic steadily as new motorway links have permitted faster running.

In view of this enthusiasm, it is rather strange that the company has shown little interest in inter-urban limited-stop routes of the kind developed by Northern, an omission all the more conspicuous in view of the vast improvement in trunk roads in the North East in recent years, which makes traditional bus routes look very slow. The company's apparent policy of making each route serve as many communities as possible, while successful in giving a wide range of point-to-point facilities, results in detours which make bus travel over any distance unattractive. For example, three routes run between Durham and Hartlepool, which by the main road are 18 miles apart, but the shortest journey time is 83min. One would expect that where the rail service has been withdrawn and a frequent but slow bus service exists, with new motorways (Newcastle-Blyth for example), there should be a market for a regular fast link, perhaps at the expense of some existing journeys.

A solitary limited-stop route from Darlington to Crook introduced as a rail replacement was abandoned in 1971, and apart from this only a few journeys have been run, for workers and Saturday shoppers, in South Northumberland and on Teesside. However, after extensive market research in Cramlington (a subject in which, again, United set the standard for other companies) a regular limited-stop was introduced from the town to Newcastle in 1974, and in the following year the Newcastle–Ashington–Newbiggin express was strengthened at the expense of the stopping service.

2

THE NORTHERN GENERAL GROUP

Beginnings: Gateshead, Tynemouth and Jarrow Tramways

The British Electric Traction Company was registered in London in 1896, its aim 'to develop electric traction in the UK and overseas'. From the beginning its managing director, Emile Garcke, had the ambitious objective of controlling as many of the rapidly growing number of urban tramway systems as possible, both by construction and by taking over existing businesses. One of its first purchases, in 1897, was of the Gateshead and District Tramways Co, which started running steam trams in 1883 over four short routes within the borough.

Gateshead has always been something of a poor relation of Newcastle, on the opposite bank of the Tyne. Dr Johnson's description of it as 'a dirty lane leading to Newcastle' is well known, and for good measure John Wesley considered its inhabitants to be a multitude of sinners – apparently influenced by the number of public houses (still considerable) in the High Street. It could never pretend to be other than an industrial town, with an emphasis on engineering. Hearse remarked 'Much of the town is congested and formed of old property: the main streets are steep, some having a gradient of 1 in 8' and the principal change one would observe now is the demolition of much of the town centre, partly to accommodate traffic on the Great North Road which speeds towards Newcastle over the rooftops of 'unlovely' Gateshead.

Such a densely populated, essentially working-class area clearly offered opportunities in public transport. BET set about obtaining an Act of Parliament, passed in 1899, to increase the number of routes and to electrify them all. The resulting seven routes were to the suburbs of Heworth, Low Fell, Dunston, Wrekenton, Bensham, Saltwell Park and Teams, and all radiated from the town centre near the river crossing; the line to Teams was a shuttle service run by one tram.

The Gateshead system was an early exponent of simple fares.

It originally cost 1d for any journey, but the management was not too happy about this, particularly on the Wrekenton route which was three miles long; from about 1910 the 'fair fare' was introduced here, as it had been in other BET subsidiaries; in this case it involved a charge of $\frac{1}{4}$d per stop. There were not, though, financial problems at Gateshead, for the network was always very profitable, paying a dividend of 7 per cent in 1910 and 10 per cent in 1921.

Meanwhile, in 1899, BET had also gained control of a steam tramway on the north bank of the Tyne, but nine miles eastward, at its mouth. The North Shields & Tynemouth District Tramways Co in 1890 was the third to operate trams between the towns in its title, the first two having failed; when BET took over, the name was again changed to the Tynemouth & District Electric Traction Co. Electrification, and a widening of the gauge from 3ft to 3ft 6in, were immediately undertaken and from 1901 a service was introduced from the New Quay in North Shields through Tynemouth to Whitley Bay, where the line was extended in 1904.

The coastal towns of Tynemouth and Whitley Bay, since being connected by railway with Newcastle, had become recognised as dormitory towns for the middle classes from the city, and at Tynemouth a station of suitable Victorian dignity and extravagance had been built for the purpose. To a lesser extent they had also emerged as seaside playgrounds, a role which was to be increased enormously by the accessibility and cheapness of the trams. BET regarded it as a sign that the tram had overcome public suspicion, and certainly that it could take traffic from the railways, when in 1903 a party of 700 made the journey from Wallsend to Whitley Bay by Tynemouth trams, under the auspices of the 'Hope of Wallsend Tent of Juvenile Rechabites'. As six of the company's largest cars wound their way through Wallsend the residents lined the streets, attracted by the excited yells of the children; a better advertisement could hardly be imagined.

The industrial activity of the River Tyne extended along the south bank as well as the north, and BET was keen to repeat the success of its Gateshead operation. Indeed, the long term aim was to have a continuous tramway from Gateshead to South Shields and thence to Sunderland. Jarrow, midway between Gateshead and South Shields, seemed to offer potential and in

1903 the Jarrow & District Electric Traction Co Ltd was incorporated, starting operations at the end of 1906.

This undertaking consisted of a line from the western end of Jarrow, traversing the town and ending just inside the County Borough of South Shields at Tyne Dock, where it connected with Corporation trams to the town centre. The single route was considered unsatisfactory locally, not only because of a desire for a more extensive service but because it was thought less suitable to become part of a through Gateshead–Shields route than a more southerly line also authorised. The section between Jarrow and the Gateshead terminus at Heworth lay in the area of Hebburn UDC, which was very keen to see the trams, but had lost the opportunity to force BET to construct a line. The Gateshead company was now only prepared to run if Hebburn Council laid the tracks first, and here the parties stuck; the link was never made.

In the opposite direction progress was little better. In June 1908 Jarrow tramcars began running through to South Shields pier head, an agreement having been made to pay over the fares collected to South Shields Corporation, after deducting running expenses. However, the two operators could not agree what those expenses should be, and after only three years the many workers travelling between Jarrow and Shields once more had to get used to waiting in the rain at Tyne Dock.

Growth of the Companies to 1926

In an Act of Parliament of 1909 the Gateshead company obtained powers to run motor buses. They were to be used for the role often assigned to buses at the time, to provide a feeder service from outer tram termini to areas where the density of traffic would not justify extending the tracks. The first route, opened in May 1913, ran southwards from the Low Fell terminus along the Great North Road to Chester-le-Street, and was so successful that within a month it was extended a further seven miles to Durham; a through fare of 1s (5p) from Gateshead to Durham was offered. Encouraged, the company then introduced similar services from the Heworth terminus to Fatfield (south of Washington) and to Jarrow. Hebburn Council, having lost its chance with the trams, immediately instructed its surveyor to improve the roads to make the connection possible!

It was the policy of BET, where it had various tramway interests in a conurbation and was developing bus services between them, to create an umbrella holding company to co-ordinate the various interests. Thus, on 29 November 1913 the Northern General Transport Co was registered, and shareholders in the three tramway companies were offered Northern shares in exchange. The Gateshead bus routes were taken over from 1 January 1914 by the new company, which operated its 27 buses from a garage and headquarters in Chester-le-Street, and within the year a further depot was opened at Stanley.

The outbreak of the first world war put an end to ideas of rapid expansion. Staff were enlisted in the forces and some vehicles requisitioned, so that an immediate pre-war fleet of 54 was reduced to 26 and the number of routes from 13 to 5.

After 1918 the company fought back, and using the best resources in terms of rolling stock it could obtain (mostly of military origin) the magic figure of 100 buses was reached in 1922, spread over 15 routes. The headquarters and central works moved from Chester-le-Street, partly a mining centre but also a pleasant market town with pastoral views over the River Wear, to Bensham, a smoky suburb of unlovely Gateshead. One imagines this must have caused some regrets among the management staff who had to move; most of the financial staff, however, have remained at Chester-le-Street to the present day, where the depot has been expanded progressively over the years. Bensham also became an operating garage from 1924.

Now came the era of unparalleled expansion in the bus business before the general strike of 1926 and subsequent depression damaged the economy of Tyneside and inevitably restrained even a growth industry. In 1924 alone Northern, having largely forgotten its tramway feeder origins, opened further depots at Consett and Sunderland, increased the fleet to 172, and ran its first extended tour, a seven-day Scottish holiday following the success of day tours introduced three years earlier. The year also saw the first recorded take-over of a rival operator, the Crescent Company, which had been running over the original route from Gateshead to Durham. Northern, conscious of competition on this route more than others, and probably understating the situation, described Crescent as 'a thorn in its flesh'. In the following year (1925) the unfortunately-titled Invincible company was taken over, which ran southwards from Sunderland to the mining district of Seaham; this led to the opening of a further depot in Murton to serve the area.

So far, so good; but the need which had stood out above all others was for a service across the Tyne from Gateshead into Newcastle. In the early 1920s all Northern routes stopped short in Gateshead because the only suitable crossing was on the lower deck of Stephenson's famous High Level railway bridge, owned by the North Eastern Railway. That company had fixed a toll of $\frac{1}{2}$d per foot passenger and 4d for a vehicle pulled by a single horse, which led an enterprising horse-bus operator, T. Howe, to the natural assumption that people would rather pay $\frac{1}{2}$d to be carried over the bridge than pay the same to walk. The NER could find no legal means of ending the loss to itself brought about by this service, universally known as the 'Ha'penny Lop', and it continued at that time to be the only form of road passenger transport across the Tyne.

For several years the Gateshead Company, Newcastle Corporation and the NER argued about the suitability of the High Level bridge for various types of traffic and who should provide the service. In 1920 Newcastle secured an Act of Parliament giving authority to construct a tramway across the bridge and proceeded to lay down tracks. Three years later through tram operation commenced, with Gateshead and Newcastle cars running jointly from southern to northern suburbs; passengers paid a surcharge of $\frac{1}{2}$d on the fare, which was passed on (by this time) to the London & North Eastern Railway. Northern buses began running across the river, and a small bus station was built at the southern end of the bridge in Gateshead, opposite the terminus of the Ha'penny Lop, which survived until 1933.

The group's buses also appeared in Northumberland under the 'Tynemouth' fleet name. Unlike Gateshead and Jarrow which confined themselves to their tram routes, the Tynemouth company pioneered bus routes on the north bank of the Tyne and along the coast to Blyth, an area where United was growing simultaneously. In 1925 the original tram depot at Cullercoats was supplemented by new premises at Percy Main, between Wallsend and North Shields, which was to become the headquarters of the Tynemouth company.

John Petrie: General Manager, 1926–1936

The year 1926 is remembered by the Northern Group not only as the year of the general strike but as that in which the first general manager, R. W. Cramp, was succeeded by John Petrie. In the next decade, thanks only in part to the Road Traffic Act of 1930, the Northern Group was to emerge in a form which remained substantially the same for 40 years, and it was to establish a particular reputation for engineering originality.

Petrie had been a protegé of L. G. Wyndham Shire, a 'great pioneer of operating engineers' who was chief engineer of the Birmingham & Midland Motor Omnibus Co (Midland Red), a BET subsidiary. Before we can appreciate the importance of Shire's and Petrie's contributions, we should remind ourselves of the kind of bus normally being used at the time. In 1922 'the fleet consisted, on paper, of approximately 100 vehicles. All were single-deckers, although when services started they were operated with CC-type Daimler double-deckers taken from the London streets. It follows, therefore, that they had open tops. They did not have a very long innings. An unfortunate passenger, having elected to stand up when approaching a low bridge, paid the penalty by getting a nasty knock on the head. This incident determined the company to discontinue the use of double-deck vehicles.'

Initially the double-deck bodies were scrapped and replaced by Bensham-built rear-entrance single-deck bodies. 'When fully laden, which meant getting in as many passengers packed in as closely as sardines in a tin as the bus would hold, there was so much weight behind the back axle that it was only now and again that the four wheels touched the road'. This was clearly unsatisfactory, and Northern dispatched a young ex-army engineer, G. W. Hayter, to Slough, then the army dump of the 1914–18 war, with instructions to buy 100 Y-type AEC lorries. Northern then rebuilt the frame and mounted its own 32-seat body on it: 'compared to other vehicles of its time it looked enormous and immediately was christened by the drivers *Big Bertha*'.

By the mid-1920s Northern was suffering considerably from independent competition – the pirates, who maintained no fixed timetable and, thanks to running light, fast buses, could literally run rings around the ponderous military cast-offs. For all BET's supercilious criticism of the 'jitneys' as cheap and nasty, the fact

45

was that their performance was superior. Wyndham Shire's response to this was to evolve a custom-built bus named the SOS; weighing only 3 tons 15 cwt, it carried 32 passengers in comfort and gave a fuel consumption of 8–10 mpg.

Not surprisingly, Petrie brought the Birmingham product with him, and Northern's review of its role in later years was lyrical. 'Light, fast and comfortable, it played a bigger part in the elimination of competition than any previous efforts. For the first time it was possible to acquire a chassis specially designed from stem to stern to carry passengers on pneumatic tyres.' The SOS became the standard bus at Northern and Tynemouth, and by the early 1930s most of the fleet were of that type. One of the last, delivered in 1934, was described in 1946 as 'still good for the mileage to the moon and back'. By 1929 the fleet had grown to 300, the Big Berthas still being in use, but 'running on routes reasonably free from the competition of the light, fast vehicles'!

However, Petrie had plans for his competitors. He recalled later: 'R. J. Howley, my chairman, said (in 1926, when he took over) he agreed with a takeover policy and then left it to me. Of course, we had to be careful not to upset United Automobile Services, a much bigger company than Northern General, and in quite a few cases it would mean a joint takeover to be divided between the two of us.'

The burden on the High Level bridge between Newcastle and Gateshead was relieved in 1928 by the opening of the Tyne bridge. Tram tracks were laid across it, giving a second route for the joint Corporation/Gateshead services, and Northern opened its own bus station in the city in Worswick Street, a strategic site close both to the centre and the new main access route. Tynemouth also extended its Blyth-Wallsend route through to Gateshead and, cut back to Whitley Bay, it was to be the first route worked by both the subsidiary and the Northern parent company.

The Railway (Road Transport) Acts were passed in 1928. Negotiations between BET and the railways were less complex than in the case of the still-independent United, and resulted in the LNER taking one share less than BET in the Northern company. Those of the LNER's road services in the Durham area within Northern's territory, as agreed with United (page 24), were taken over, the principal one being from Durham to Sacriston. It is interesting that in this area railway traffic had been lost, not only to the numerous independent bus operators, but possibly also to the LNER buses themselves; the station-master at Witton Gilbert commented in his returns for 1928 that 'passenger traffic is adversely affected by increased bus services from here to Newcastle, Chester-le-Street, South Shields, Consett and Durham, etc'. Northern had also been responsible, in 1922, for the abandonment of the NER's South Shields – Harton bus service.

Railway association brought into Northern control several small operators bought out by the LNER in the few months before the Acts, of which two, having survived the takeover for some years, are of particular interest. The General County Omnibus Co, which had been formed in 1927 and ran three important routes: Newcastle–Durham–Middlesbrough, Newcastle–Chester-le-Street–Waterhouses, and also South Shields–Esh Winning; in 1931, *after takeover by Northern*, General County acquired G. W. Hetherington's A1 Autombile Services, running from Bishop Auckland to Sunderland and South Shields and to Newcastle. These latter were merged with Northern and United services, but General County continued running, its buses in Northern livery until 1936, when it was absorbed and United took over the southern end of the Middlesbrough route. We may surmise that Northern's reason for retaining a separate company was to avoid having to hand over part to United under the territorial agreement, as United was to do in reverse with its Durham District associate 20 years later.

The second business, that of Thomas Wakefield, was to have a still longer history. A new high-standard road from Newcastle to the Northumberland coast, opened in 1927, induced Wakefield to begin running from Tynemouth to the city, jointly with the Northern subsidiary; a third partner, in the form of Newcastle Corporation, was to join the following year. In March 1928 a further route to Newcastle, from Wakefield's headquarters at North Shields, was introduced and the absorption of a joint operator on this, Archer Brothers, brought local North Shields and Wallsend routes. Rapid expansion of services over the next year, typical of the period immediately before the Road Traffic Act, was brought to an end by transfer of the shares to Northern in November 1929.

The Tynemouth company had introduced a further service

along the coast road in 1928 and by now it was clear that its future was in buses rather than trams. Buses began to run over the tram route from April 1930 and conversion was completed in August 1931, involving a rationalisation of Wakefield's operations in North Shields. In view of the very close relationship between Wakefield's and the larger company, now renamed the Tynemouth & District Transport Company, it is remarkable that the Wakefield name survived; probably it would not have done in a group not endowed with a tradition of numerous subsidiaries. Operations were concentrated on the Percy Main depot and henceforward all coaches were to be 'Wakefield's', although the insignia appeared on a few buses too.

The Tynemouth company tramway was not the first to be abandoned, for the distinctions of being the last on Tyneside to open and the first to close both fell to Jarrow, a system which never had much chance, given the attitude of the South Shields tramways committee. Following pressure from the local press, the Jarrow–Shields through service had been resumed in 1922, but was abandoned again in 1927. Undoubtedly this was partly because in the previous July Northern had applied to South Shields Watch Committee for licences in respect of 25 buses, under the pre-1930 system, to run between Gateshead and Shields over the tram route. Against the recommendation of the tramways committee, the application had been granted. Local unemployment was having a damaging effect on revenue, and with a through bus service there was no reason to retain the trams; accordingly preparations were made for abandonment on 30 June 1929. Northern opened a further depot, in South Shields, to cater for the Jarrow traffic, and so this was to be the only case within the Group where buses of the parent company, rather than a subsidiary, replaced trams. In fact for a year the Northern buses ran on hire to Jarrow & District, after which the company lay dormant and was finally dissolved in 1948.

The Road Traffic Act of 1930 did not, in the short term, have the profound effect on Northern that it achieved elsewhere. The fleet, which stood at 321 after the Jarrow conversion, had only reached 380 by 1931, about an average year's growth, despite the takeover of independents. This was partly because some were, in the sense of the Act, 'unnecessary', ie the total traffic could be carried in a smaller fleet, to which the depression must also have made its contribution; it was also partly because,

NUMBER ONE: South Shields' first municipal bus was battery powered, introduced in 1914 and evocatively known as the Red Sardine.

Tyne & Wear PTE

NUMBER ONE: O.S. Gibson, proprietor of Weardale Motor Services, ushers a patriarchal customer into his first vehicle. *Weardale Motor Services*

Marlborough Crescent bus station, Newcastle, in the late 1920s. In the centre a London-style AEC of Newcastle Corporation Blue Bus fleet; left and right, Renaults of the opposition, the Blaydon 'A' co-operative.

Collection of G.E. Hutchinson

Venture, as most will remember the company. A spotless Leyland Leopard runs through inhospitable country between Consett and Blanchland. *C.S. Marshall*

when acquired vehicles were examined, they were often found to be dangerously unroadworthy. We may imagine that when one fleet was bought out, which is remembered as being managed by a superintendent and inspector previously sacked by Northern, its days were numbered.

In the calmer and more assured atmosphere of the 1930s, Petrie, together with Major Hayter, now his chief engineer, evolved his chef d'oeuvre, the successor to the SOS. Northern's problem in the coming years was to be not so much of competition as of capacity, yet most single deck buses available seated no more than 35. In many places low bridges prevented the use of double deckers, and in any case Hayter 'would like to state that while he regards the double-decker as eminently suited for riding from Oxford Circus to the Marble Arch, he does not regard it as a vehicle for inter-urban provincial services unless the services are so heavy that a 60-seater vehicle is required'.

The answer to Northern's problem was the SE6, a single-decker built 'with no other object than that of providing the maximum seating accommodation within the regulation overall dimensions'. Built at Bensham to be the standard bus of the 1930s, the SE6 achieved the then remarkable number of 45 seats, by moving the engine from its traditional position at the front to the side. Even then, the object was only secured by using a very shallow engine with side valves, and American Hercules units were used. SE4s were also built – the difference lay in the number of wheels – and from the first SE6 in 1933 these strange buses became Northern's mainstay until after the war. The large-capacity single decker was to be a distinguishing characteristic of Northern until the arrival of the 30ft underfloor-engined single-decker in the early 1950s, although in later years a compromise was found by using conventional buses and squeezing the driver's cab into less than the usual space.

With the SE6 in widespread use, Petrie departed in 1936, leaving G. W. Hayter to be general manager. He was to be remembered not only as an engineer but as a gentleman and supreme diplomat; it is recorded that, in the difficult times of the late 1920s he was the only manager who could successfully negotiate a cut in wages. He also believed in mastering everything personally, including conducting his own cases in traffic courts.

Petrie was widely travelled; between Midland Red and Northern he had worked for undertakings in Madrid and Shanghai, and his heart was in a remote part of the French Pyrenees. He now decided, at the age of 56, to realise his ideal of retiring there before he was too old, although he was to return to BET in England during the second world war.

SDO and Tyneside: More Subsidiaries

During his stewardship Petrie added two more ex-tramway companies to the Northern family. In 1903 the United Kingdom Tramways, Light Railways & Electrical Syndicate had started a tramway which, when completed in 1906, ran from the Sunderland Corporation terminus at Grangetown through a series of mining villages to Herrington Burn and Houghton-le-Spring, with branches to Penshaw, Fencehouses and Easington Lane. The proprietors of the Sunderland District Electric Tramways Co, as one might suppose from their grandiose title, had ideas of following the BET lead, but most of their projects were ill-conceived; one in Essex, to connect Southend and Colchester by a route which included a ferry, can only be called mad. The nature of the Sunderland system was essentially inter-urban, whereas all successful networks were within towns, and its poor traffic, together with local industrial troubles, was to be its undoing.

Bankruptcy, following a Wearside shipbuilders' strike in 1909, brought in a receiver in 1913, who was able to improve finances, not, however, to the extent that the ordinary shareholders ever received a dividend. In this dire position, the company declined to pay a wage award to its staff which the National Industrial Council recommended in 1920, and when two years later a national agreement reduced some wages by 3s (15p) a week, Sunderland District men were asked to accept a further cut of 10s (50p). The management's response to the strike which inevitably followed was to threaten the use of blackleg labour, but the declared intention of the mineworkers, who constituted most of the passengers, to boycott the trams prevented this proposal. The unhappy industrial relations of the group in later years cannot be blamed entirely on the trade unions.

By this time the trams were becoming vulnerable to bus

52

competition, especially since the main tram route from Houghton to Grangetown, later to be that of SDO bus No 111, was indirect. To make matters worse, Sunderland Corporation had refused to allow through running over its tracks to the centre of Sunderland, making a change necessary; the Corporation relented in 1921, bringing some benefit, though only temporary. It was decided to go over to bus operation from 1924, and by July the following year conversion was completed – but the company, now renamed Sunderland District Transport Company as entry into the road haulage business was contemplated, was not yet out of the wood. The coal strike of 1926 brought the receiver in a second time, and success only came after a second financial reconstruction. Now the Sunderland District Omnibus Co (to be known universally as SDO) took over two smaller operators itself and expanded its routes before passing into the Northern group in 1931.

Reorganisation of Northern and SDO routes within the Gateshead/Durham/Sunderland triangle followed, with many joint services, so that the depot at Philadelphia, near Houghton-le-Spring, became virtually another Northern base, running blue buses rather than red. In this geographical position there was bound to be a continuing dependence on the mining industry, leading management to comment in 1948:

> The company's services operate mainly in the colliery districts around Houghton-le-Spring, and as long as the miners' wages remain at their present high level the prosperity of the company is assured, always provided there are no serious increases in the rates of pay for transport workers.

There was then evidently little fear of busmen becoming miners, or miners buying cars, or of the collieries closing.

In Northumberland, the much smaller Tyneside Tramways and Tramroads Company had entered business in 1902 with a line from North Shields to Wallsend, where it turned North to skirt the suburbs of Newcastle and terminate in Gosforth. At Wallsend Tyneside's lines joined those of Newcastle Corporation (NCT), making a through North Shields–Newcastle service technically possible, although initially NCT resisted the granting of running powers. Tyneside sought Parliamentary authority and came close enough to obtaining it to worry NCT, which compromised by allowing company cars to run through to Newcastle in return for its use of Tyneside track in Gosforth. In the years after 1904, as Hearse recalls, 'From the boundary at Wallsend a Corporation conductor replaced his Tyneside confrère and took all the fares, less an allowance of 2d a mile. The Tyneside driver got a higher rate of pay on the Corporation section, which was always called 'Stanhope money', because the service ran to Stanhope Road in West Newcastle'.

Tyneside went over to buses in 1930 and was still running its two routes when absorbed in 1936. Close co-ordination with NCT continued, the two using a common terminus in Croft Street, Newcastle, for buses which the operators ran alternately as far as Wallsend. It was only in 1965 that the title was changed to the Tyneside Omnibus Company.

The War and After: G. W. Hayter

In the late 1930s the North East began to respond to Government policies to improve the employment situation, and as the pattern of industrial activity changed, so did that of the Northern Companies' services. In particular, the acquisition in 1937 of the last independent operator on South Tyneside, Charlton of Hebburn, led to reorganisation in the area, and one of the principal instruments of the unemployment policy was to be a large trading estate at Team Valley, south-west of Gateshead and therefore served entirely by Northern group buses.

The principal effect of the second world war was to continue trends already being experienced. Employment at Team Valley increased from 5,000 to 14,000, of whom 90 per cent were carried on 500 Northern journeys every day; services have continued to carry about 7,000 a day, especially from Newcastle and the West Durham mining villages, and there are few communities in the area without a direct service. Also in Durham, the Royal Ordnance Factory at Birtley required 350 journeys and the expansion of shipbuilding around Jarrow 200, while on the opposite bank 120 journeys were required to Wallsend. This was achieved despite the mobilisation of 1,000 employees and the requisition of 90 buses, replaced by only 26 new ones in the six years. It proved possible, however, to use the war effort to relieve Northern of part of its low bridge problem. Two of the most important, in terms of vehicle use, were on the approach to Worswick Street bus station in Newcastle, and the arches at Tyne Dock under railway lines which led to the coal staithes; pleading a saving in fuel and manpower, Hayter persuaded the highway authorities to *widen* the footpath in each case, creating a narrow but clear passage in the middle for double-deckers.

Hardly was the war over when BET faced the threat of nationalisation, which was much talked about and finally appeared as inevitable in the area schemes of 1949. British Electric Traction, always a stout defender of the capitalist system, thus had to defend its principles in the North East, since Northern would be the first company to be involved. 'It does not make sense,' thundered Major Hayter, 'and one can only assume that the ideology of the nationalisation enthusiasts has run away with them.'

Why was the area chosen? It has been argued that it was because to some extent the area was already served by United, state-owned since Tilling's decision to sell, an action which BET felt as a slap in the face. Fulford observed: 'If BET had trotted torpidly in the wake of Tilling, the story of the Government's attempts to take over road passenger transport must have had a different ending'. Things were to be otherwise 20 years later. However even in 1950 BET would no doubt have been prepared to sell, at the right price for a period of growth.

It is also suggested that in the area 'rural and urban were nicely balanced', but this could apply to many parts of the country. More probably Whitehall under-estimated the resistance of BET and the Labour-controlled municipal operators, whose efforts were much appreciated by BET. There were also, of course, many independent firms, and Hayter quickly organised a meeting between them in Newcastle which, addressed by the Chairman of BET, succeeded in achieving a united front. The general manager was described as 'indefatigable' in his attempts to ensure that everyone knew the effect of the scheme as BET saw it; buses went on their way covered with slogans making uncomplimentary remarks about the cost of nationalised transport.

The fleet strength in 1947 stood at:

Northern	554
SDO	109

Tynemouth	56
Tyneside	23
Wakefield	11

and, in Gateshead, 76 trams. This was not only the last of Northern's tram operations but one of the last company tram undertakings in the country. Conversion to trolleybuses had already been contemplated, notably in 1938 under the Gateshead & District Tramways and Trolley Vehicles Act, when the outbreak of war prevented implementation. The political uncertainties of the late 1940s made BET reluctant to act, but once the immediate danger of a wasted investment seemed to be out of the way, an Act of Parliament was promoted in 1950. As would have been the case in 1938, conversion had to be dovetailed with NCT's plans and took place in stages between 5 March 1950 and 4 August 1951; as befitted the occasion, the last tram was driven by the chairman of BET, severing its last link with the business that had brought the Group its prosperity. Buses of the new Gateshead & District Omnibus Co took over and, for the first time, NCT buses ran into Gateshead. It now became possible to extend the 'tram' routes, which had not been changed for many years, into the housing estates which were fast growing on the southern outskirts, whereas between the wars new services had been provided by Northern buses; probably this was to protect the group from the effects of the Gateshead Acts which, like most involving company tramways, gave the local authority a right to purchase after a given number of years. However, the Gateshead buses, running from the old tram depot in Sunderland Road, continued to be entirely separate operationally and organisationally from those of Northern, based at Bensham.

With the political climate more favourable, Northern also set about purchasing more independent businesses. The most important were those of J. W. Hurst of Winlaton, in the outer south-western suburbs of Tyneside (1951), which led to the opening of a further depot, and of Bee-Line Continental Tours in 1957; this was to assist in the build-up of an enterprise which had begun three years earlier.

Hayter, the last of Northern's engineer–general managers, whose forceful personality had steered the company through the war and the nationalisation threat to a period of stability, retired in 1954; appropriately the last SE6 ran at the same time. It is said that on being asked by a bodybuilder with what he would like the seats of some new buses covered he snorted 'Arses, of course', a comment which sums up Northern's marketing approach.

1954 – 1968: J. W. Forster

Hayter gave way to a company-bred traffic man. James Forster had been a clerk at Stanley in 1922 at the age of 18, and had opened Consett depot as traffic superintendent two years later; after being traffic manager between periods with the Lincolnshire and Trent Companies, he now returned to the top post. Policy over the next years was to be based on obtaining for Northern the maximum possible share of the total market; rather than allow a competitor to take on some new business, it was ensured that Northern had first claim, even though it might mean finding an additional bus and crew which would be idle for most of the day.

This, naturally, amounted to a declaration of war on the independent operators, and the issue was one which strained the relationship with United. That company was generally prepared to co-exist with its smaller neighbours; the difference in attitude did not matter so far as the territories were self-contained, but there were two ambitious independents, OK and Trimdon Motor Services, based in the United area and running important routes over the Durham/Easington frontier. It did not help, either, that Durham District Services, virtually United buses in disguise, were on the wrong side of the line, notably on the main road south from Sunderland.

A more positive development was the introduction, at the end of the decade, of inter-urban limited stop services. The frequent journeys between the main towns required duplication during the morning and evening peak, and surveys showed a high proportion of longer-distance passengers; there was also an awareness of loss of business to the railways and the private car. On four of these routes – Newcastle to Durham, South Shields, and Sunderland, and Sunderland to Durham – hourly express workings were introduced in September 1959, replacing peak hour duplicates and making use of the vehicles all day. Over the next decade advantage was taken of major road improvements in Co Durham, a result of government regional policies, to

57

maintain the attractiveness of the services. New routes were introduced, first, in May 1961, from Sunderland to Consett (this one not competing with rail), then, in October 1965, a shorter route from Newcastle to Winlaton, and, in February 1966, from Newcastle to Hartlepool, bringing in SDO and United as joint operators. Another route, joint with United, from Ashington to Stanley via Newcastle, began in 1970, and from October 1969 a similarly trans-urban route ran across Sunderland from Jarrow to Seaham.

The limited-stop routes have been a commendable attempt to improve the competitiveness of the bus, which has been appreciated by the public; their main weakness has been a tendency, despite a general policy of using coaches, for standee single-deckers and even double-deckers to appear.

History repeated itself in March 1961 when Northern opened a depot in Jarrow, principally to avoid running empty buses into the town from depots elsewhere for local routes to new estates on the outskirts. Jarrow was growing in response to Government attempts to bring new industry to the area but also, indirectly, because of the Durham planning policy of concentrating new industry in the eastern half of the county. Apart from particular black spots like Jarrow where high unemployment needed attention, growth was to be concentrated in new towns, of which one lay within Northern's territory. A few miles south of Jarrow and just outside the Tyneside conurbation is Washington, where a position between Tyneside and Wearside, closeness to the A1 Motorway and local colliery closures made it an ideal centre for new industry. By 1968 a base was necessary here too, which made local routes possible and, like Jarrow, took over some buses from other depots; within five years Washington had a fleet of 40 vehicles.

By comparison with most other large bus companies, one-man operation was very slow to be accepted in the Northern group. It is difficult to say whether this was attributable more to the trade union or management side. On the one hand we remember the militant tradition of Tyneside and the importance of maintaining employment to the home of the Jarrow Crusade; on the other Northern was still a generally prosperous company operating busy services. At any rate, the first one-man bus ran in 1967 on the quiet Houghton-le-Spring to Seaham route, from Murton depot, and was soon followed by routes at Philadelphia

(SDO) and Consett. The Gateshead fleet ran only double-deckers, and in order to implement the policy there it was necessary to rebuild some existing buses with centre doors; Jarrow and Wallsend (Tyneside) were also to introduce conductor-less double deckers over the following few years.

After the SE6 type buses Northern had followed very much the normal vehicle policy of the BET group. In 1959 the Leyland Atlantean, a double-deck innovation which moved the engine to the back and the entrance forward of the front axle (and thus suitable for one-man operation) became available in quantity and the Northern Companies joined many of their BET associates in taking advantage of its higher capacity. For five years the Atlantean was standard, but then a most surprising change was made. London Transport's custom-built bus, the short, rear-entrance Routemaster, regarded elsewhere as old-fashioned, was developed into an experimental larger forward-entrance version (still with the engine at the front), and Northern ordered 50. They were to be the only Routemasters bought new outside London. The original experimental bus was not developed for London use but in fact was sold to Northern. Route-masters were regarded as particularly suitable for the longer inter-urban services and all remained with the parent company, although they were to be used fairly indiscriminately; the subsidiaries, with their generally shorter routes, stayed faithful to the Atlantean and the similar Daimler Fleetline. Northern also returned to convention later, but its faith in the Routemaster was to be justified, for experience showed that a price, in loss of reliability, had to be paid for the rear-engined layout; a major overhaul for an Atlantean cost three times as much.

An era was about to end. A Labour Government was again in power, whose widely circulated plans for conurbation transport authorities sounded very like the area schemes of 1949. The White Paper 'Public Transport and Traffic' published in 1966 did not spell out 'nationalisation', but the interested parties were not discouraged from drawing such a conclusion, and no party was more interested than BET. Once more posters on buses invited the public to oppose the intended legislation, but behind the scenes the BET Board was taking stock. Whereas in 1949 the industry still had a few boom years to enjoy, by now there was indisputable evidence of decline. BET had already diversified into such areas as laundries and Rediffusion, and there seemed little point in letting political ideals lead to financial loss; the Group had built its fortunes not only on perceiving areas of potential growth, but on pulling out when profits were no longer there, and, for the very respectable price of £35m all BET's British bus interests were sold in November 1967 to the Transport Holding Company.

The Northern Group entered 1969 not only as a state-owned business, but with a new breed of General Manager in L. S. Higgins, an Oxford man who had once been assistant traffic manager. He set about accelerating the introduction of one-man buses and ending some of the 'old Spanish customs'; typically, in 1969 the 'Wakefield' name gave way to 'Tynemouth' on bus and coach sides, though bus passengers were still recommended on tickets:

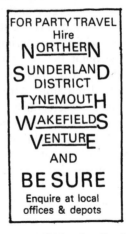

Venture? We must now fit in the final piece of the jig-saw.

The Venture Transport Company

This was the largest independent business in the North East. Its origins can be traced to Messrs Harper and Lockey, who after the first world war began running from Shotley Bridge, near Consett, to Newcastle with the ubiquitous converted army trucks. Later the business was sold to G. R. Harrison and W. T. Richardson of Hamsterley Colliery; they introduced the 'Venture' fleetname with the blessing of a local coal-owner who used the name for his four-in-hand, and in 1929 the business became a limited company under the name of Venture Bus Services Ltd.

Before 1914 the five Reed brothers of Sunniside had added to their garage business a bus which they ran to the Bensham tram terminus. In 1918 they recommenced with two Albions, which ran from Newcastle to Chopwell over substantially the same route as Harper and Lockey, and the two parties joined forces in 1925 when they extended the Shotley Bridge route into Consett. The decision to make Consett the centre of operations, where the steelworks and associated industry were to be important sources of traffic, was taken when in 1929 Reed Brothers bought land and buildings at Blackhill which were to remain the headquarters, although the association between the two firms remained informal for another year. With a formal licensing structure ahead they then decided to operate jointly and to pool receipts; the fleetname 'Venture and Reed Bros' was now used, although the vehicles were individually owned and licensed. Regulation also made it worth taking over other businesses, and Reed Bros bought a Consett–Blanchland route from Walker of Edmundbyers and two routes to Newcastle from J. Clydesdale of Chopwell, while J. R. & R. B. Parker, who ran jointly with Clydesdale on the same routes, sold to Venture.

The rapid development of these services did considerable damage to railway traffic in the area, where the stations were often distant from the communities they served. The Derwent Valley line from Newcastle to Consett, which flanked the bus route, lost a third of its passengers between 1919 and 1921, and, as bus services continued to improve, the worst-placed of the stations lost three-quarters of their remaining trade by 1934. By this time a business of 25 vehicles had become a joint subsidiary with the name of Robson Bros Ltd, of which one branch gave a further Consett-Newcastle route, and the other, known as the Yellow Bus Service, was based at High Spen with a group of routes in that area. Yellow Bus remained separate and, together with another small business in High Spen, purchased in 1934, led to the establishment of Venture's second depot in that village.

The proprietors then turned to improving the fleets and developing new routes, of which two, to Stanhope and Hexham, were rural and never very successful; others, in Consett itself and the mining area to the north-east, involved Northern as joint operators. The organisation clearly needed tidying up, and in 1938 a new private limited company, Venture Transport Co (Newcastle) Ltd was created, which was half owned by the Reed family and half by the Harrisons and Richardsons, who still controlled the original Venture.

After the second world war the company did well with its existing routes and extended the network, although most of the new routes, being rural, were unsuccessful and were cut back, with only some local services in Consett surviving. Its wings spread in 1951 when the C & E Bus Co was purchased, run by Messrs Colpitt and Elwood, with 13 buses on a circular route in the urban Stanley/Dipton area. This was in Northern territory, completely detached from Venture routes, and the name was retained along with the premises; however, Venture buses immediately took over, carrying labels 'On Hire to C & E Bus Co Ltd', and this became a permanent feature. It is said that C & E first approached Northern's local Superintendent in Stanley, so that Bensham should be informed of the impending sale; no doubt Venture was able to pay a higher price.

In 1952 a process began which was to characterise future route policy. Traffic in the traditional area was declining, partly in accordance with national trends but also because in North-West Durham, where the profits had originated, collieries were closing and population declining in many of the communities served. The position of High Spen, close to the edge of the Tyneside conurbation, helped the decision to expand into the growing areas along the Tyne Valley and north of the river, so far as this would be tolerated by United. Over the next 20 years extensions to the west of Newcastle generally balanced reductions around and to the west of Consett; moreover, one-man operation was introduced in 1959 (eight years before Northern) and every route had some one-man buses, but the rate of implementation was slow. In the 1960s the business was at its peak with 85 buses.

The Transport Act of 1968 did not help Venture. Subsidies offered for rural routes were denied for all but the Blanchland route, and as a result the wild Stanhope run ceased, while the Hexham service, now cut back to Whittonstall, ran only outside peak hours. Of equal concern was the creation of the Tyneside PTE whose long-term intentions were unknown. Altogether it was an inevitable case of 'willing seller and willing buyer' when in May 1970 Venture became a Northern subsidiary. The reason for the sale was not a problem of finding a successor to take over from a pioneer, as is often the case, for it had been the policy of the Harrisons, Richardsons and Reeds, who still owned the business, to employ an independent General Manager. The last of these, Leslie Graham, had started at 14 sweeping out the garage, and was successively conductor, traffic clerk, inspector, chief inspector and traffic manager before becoming general manager in 1955.

Many enterprises like Venture have other strings to their bow; one of these, a car hire and taxi business, was taken over with the bus operations and continued under Northern control. The bus fleet was reduced by about 20 per cent as the ratio of spare buses to requirements appeared excessive, a view encouraged by current shortages in the parent fleet to which most of the surplus Venture buses were transferred. On the other hand, 'C & E' disappeared and, logically, the work was taken over by Northern's Stanley depot.

Like most Durham independents, Venture never ran a double-decker, although it is probable that the type would soon have appeared if the sale had not taken place; Consett lost the last of its passenger railway services as early as 1955 (perhaps itself evidence of Venture's efficiency), and many of the problem bridges were demolished. Again in common with others, a fleet of modern large-capacity single deckers was always run instead. In the 1930s, when Northern evolved its SE6 for the same operating conditions, Venture bought a number of similar Maudslay SF40 saloons with 40 seats; they had a conventionally mounted forward engine, but the front axle was set back behind the entrance. By the 1960s, the standard bus was a 51-seat AEC or Leyland, bodied by Alexander, to a specification suitable for hire at holiday times by United for long-distance work.

National Bus Company: 1969 onwards

In the short term there was no outward sign of the change in ownership. When, in 1970, NBC headquarters required subsidiaries to shed unremunerative rural services, it was of little significance to a group with mainly urban and inter-urban routes; however, the reluctance of Durham County Council to pay rural grants made matters more serious. No routes were completely withdrawn, although two were shortened and one reduced from daily to a Friday and Saturday service. Venture's Consett-Blanchland operation was taken over by J. Clarke of Consett, a newcomer to local buses, and, finally, the one route to receive a grant was also from Consett, but this time it was Northern's infrequent run to Tow Law. It is interesting that all the affected routes had been taken over from independents after 1939.

Of more importance to Northern was the creation, also under the 1968 Transport Act, of the Tyneside Passenger Transport Executive. That body immediately took over the Newcastle and South Shields Corporation transport undertakings, but also had a duty to provide a co-ordinated service throughout its area; this involved many of the Group's routes but particularly those of the Tyneside, Tynemouth and Gateshead companies, which ran entirely within the PTE's area. Gateshead was affected most of all. It was very unusual for local buses in a town of Gateshead's size to be run by a company rather than the municipality, in which case they would have passed automatically to the PTE; moreover, there was the very close relationship with Newcastle, for probably 95 per cent of Gateshead's mileage was on routes which were run jointly, now, with the PTE.

Thus agreement with the PTE's policies was not merely desirable but vital. The difficulty of reconciling NBC's financial requirements for the Northern Group with those policies was increased by the natural resentment of Gateshead crews at what they considered lower rewards than their PTE colleagues. Finally in 1972 an agreement was reached under which the NBC would provide services within the PTE area to its specification and at an agreed price which would cover the companies' costs, and permit pay scales to be rationalised. To make the best use of the various operators' resources (United, the Northern group and the PTE) a joint scheduling team was set up.

At this stage L. S. Higgins departed, having earned a position as chief general manager of a group of companies in the warmer south. In his place came J. B. Hargreaves, appropriately from a Tilling company, since the two groups were now merged; the wind of change blew a little more, and in 1973 Hargreaves was called to another senior post in Wales. The successor was

D. D. N. Graham, previously general manager of the York-shire Traction Co, but once a junior manager with Northern.

The most conspicuous characteristic of Northern to an outsider in the early 1970s was the continuation of the subsidiaries, each with its own livery, fare-scale and financial structure. Indeed, until about 1960 each subsidiary bought its own buses, which might be quite different from those of its fellows. While this was justified by its preservation of esprit de corps, especially at SDO and Tyneside, engineering policy has been to regard the fleets as interchangeable. One of the effects of having other than a 'company man' in J. B. Hargreaves as general manager, and of the PTE influence at the same time, was a change in liveries which introduced two new colours, but reduced the variations. NBC decreed that buses should be painted either green or poppy red, so Northern and Venture slowly changed from maroon to the latter colour, while, to establish a corporate identity with the PTE, Gateshead and Tyneside abandoned green and Tynemouth maroon, for the PTE's yellow and white. SDO, however, remained faithful to the original blue inherited from the trams. Remembering the habit of transferring buses between fleets, it is no wonder that a bewildered passenger asked an inspector in Sunderland 'Is that blue bus a green bus or a red bus?' 'Neither, madam, it's a yellow bus!'

To confuse matters further, Venture buses before the takeover were basically yellow and cream, and could easily have belonged to the PTE. It was found that fall-out from Consett Steelworks discoloured the cream roofs, and they were painted maroon until the adoption of poppy red.

Operationally little had been done over the years to rationalise the routes, except between SDO and Northern. Tyneside and Gateshead remained completely exclusive, and Tynemouth ran only a couple of routes in common with Northern depots. This laissez-faire approach was most evident in Wallsend, where local routes have always been run by Tynemouth, involving empty running from Percy Main, while the Tyneside buses, whose depot is on the spot, pass close to the Tynemouth depot. The historical explanation for this probably lies in the different gauges of the original tramways, which meant that in the early days they could not be linked; indeed, after 1945 Tynemouth buses running through Wallsend still showed NEWCASTLE

VIA TRAM ROUTE; Tynemouth trams had, of course, never reached Newcastle, but Tyneside had. Another legacy of the short Hargreaves era was an administrative reorganisation on a territorial rather than company basis, of which the first fruits appeared in 1974 when a new route was introduced, run both by Gateshead and Northern. Soon after, there were signs of the historic structure being changed more fundamentally; Northern took over the licences of SDO, Tynemouth and Venture, and the parent company name rapidly appeared on the subsidiaries' vehicles. Quite what effect this would have on colour schemes was not clear.

The total fleet had now grown to almost 1,000 buses and coaches, running from 16 depots, of which none was more than 15 miles from Bensham, quite remarkably compact for a company operator. To a large extent this reflects the densely-populated territory and low car ownership; it also results from the policy of providing frequent services and of catering for new demands as they arise. The importance of the Team Valley trading estate and Washington has already been described, while new traffic was also created by the opening of the Tyne tunnel in 1967. The Group introduced successful cross-river routes, which contrast with the earlier failure of London Transport's links through the similar Dartford–Purfleet tunnel under the Thames. Finally, as more collieries closed and work opportunities swung more from the west of Durham to the east, travelling distances to employment became longer and the assurance remained that workers' services would be important.

Not least of Northern's roles has been that of producing top management, for both the BET and NBC groups. There can be little doubt that both have consciously sent their bright men to Bensham as preparation for higher things, and equally that the experience would be an admirable background for whatever might lie ahead.

United's famous coach livery and logo originated with Orange Bros. An AEC
Regal when new in 1934, after United takeover, shows the original form.
United Automobile Services

United coach livery was not only used for coaches on the London service; sea-
front buses such as this Bristol L 'Queen Mary', on Scarborough promenade,
also used it. Scarborough's weather was thought unsuitable for the usual open-
top buses. *United Automobile Services*

A new AEC Regal for Gillett Bros crosses Framwelgate Bridge in Durham, at the foot of the Castle, in 1947. The photograph was specially posed, for Gillett's service never crossed the bridge. *British Leyland Motor Corpn*

Sunderland Corporation was one of the first operators to try fitting this style of bus for one-man operation. This Guy Arab was so altered in 1953. *Tyne & Wear PTE*

3

EAST YORKSHIRE AND KINGSTON-UPON-HULL CORPORATION

Slow Beginnings: Trams and Buses to 1926

In his book *The Rolling Road* L. A. G. Strong identifies the Hull area as one where, in the late nineteenth century, stage coaches did not entirely give way before the advancing railways, but continued to provide a network of short-stage services from the surrounding villages to the city. Most of the routes shown in Bates' directory of coaches in 1836, however, were later covered by railways, and the first *daily* service into Hull, Palframan's horse-bus from Kirk Ella, began in 1872.

By 1875 one horse-tram route was operating which, with five added later by the Hull Street Tramways Co, provided the city's basic public transport except for one route along Hedon Road, where the Drypool & Marfleet Steam Tramway Company ran steam trams. Hull Corporation took over both in 1899, and by 1903 had completed the electrification of lines along the six major roads out of the city, together with a short route to the Pier. The first motor buses appeared in 1909 to serve the Stoneferry area, inaccessible to trams on account of its narrow streets. Second-hand Saurer double-deckers were bought from the Mersey Railway Company which, although the buses were only six weeks old, had been prevented by law from using them. Their career in Hull was not long, for the operating cost of these vehicles was out of proportion to their revenue. When in 1913 the Saurer vehicles were worn out through misguided maintenance, Stoneferry lost its buses.

At this stage, and until 1919, there was no specific manager of the Corporation's transport system. Various aspects were the responsibility of the city engineer or electrical engineer, who were on a par with a third individual on the traffic side. In this situation decisions were taken by the chairman of the committee, which persisted in a tramway policy after evidence from elsewhere suggested that the tram was past its best. Although the Stoneferry bus route was reintroduced in 1921 after a long campaign and, from 1923 onwards, other buses ran, either experimentally or to new housing areas, new tram tracks were also laid until 1927 where the density of population could not justify their capital cost. Thus in 1932 Hull's internal transport system still consisted very largely of trams, the tram/bus ratio being of the order of 3:1.

BET Steps in: East Yorkshire Motor Services

Not only had the Corporation been slow to use the rapidly improving motor bus around the City, but, in the absence of a large company operator, the hinterland was not fully exploited. British Electric Traction was not slow to seize the opportunity created by this transport vacuum in setting up its own company.

East Yorkshire Motor Services is perhaps the complete opposite of Northern General, the other BET group company within the scope of this book. While Northern became very large, EYMS has remained relatively small; but more important, it is among the youngest of the group companies (dating only from 1926); its territory is largely rural, and it never had any tramway interests. The new creation was based originally on BET's purchase of two independent firms running into Hull, Lee & Beulah, and Hull & District Motors.

The first had been formed in 1921 by the amalgamation of two separate businesses, in which E. J. Lee was the predominant character. He had been employed as a coachman by a doctor in the Brough district, who bequeathed him £200, whereupon he approached another local gentleman for a loan of a further £200; with this he would purchase a charabanc, which would be fitted with a glass roof in winter. The subject of his request was the father of C. W. H. Glossop, later Conservative MP for Howdenshire, who told the story in the House of Commons in 1946 while opposing the Transport Bill which might nationalise East Yorkshire.

'My father said, "I have known you for 40 years. You are a hard working and thrifty man, but I will not lend you the £200 to put into a charabanc because you will lose your money. If you wish to put it into an ironmonger's business or a farm or a smallholding, you can have it." My father may not have realised what passenger transport might become. The man got his money, and started with his charabanc. Then he got two or three buses, and provided a service where nobody else did so.' At the time of takeover Lee & Beulah ran about 15 vehicles, principally in the Ferriby and Brough district west of Hull from a depot at Elloughton retained by EYMS, but also eastwards to Withernsea. Also retained and applied to all future East Yorkshire buses was Lee & Beulah's attractive colour scheme of dark blue and primrose.

Rather like Hull Corporation in the earlier era, the management structure of East Yorkshire in the early days is not clear. E. J. Lee became a local director at Hull, but we also come across one of the major figures in the history of BET. In 1921, when jobs were not easily found, John Spencer Wills had placed an advertisement in *The Times*, and was offered the post of private secretary at £50 per annum by Emile Garcke, managing director of BET. He was then 17 years old, and 'with commendable foresight in one so young, made it a condition of his employment that he should after two years move into the BET organisation proper.' After experience in the secretary's office at headquarters, Wills took an increasing interest in the bus operating side, and in 1926 became secretary of the new company at 22. Three years later he was secretary and joint manager, and in 1931 he returned to the BET executive staff becoming, among other things, a director of East Yorkshire.

The embryo company at first used a garage in Lister Street, Hull, but in 1928 land was purchased in Anlaby Road, one of the principal roads to the west; here a large garage was built and a house adjoining, No 252, became the registered office. Such expenditure was not out of place, for already several acquisitions had been made. All but one of these ran services radiating from Hull:

Business	Route Operated	Date of Purchase
Laidlaw Bros	Hull–Hedon	1926
Allan Lawson	Beverley–Driffield	1926
D. W. Burn	Hull–Withernsea	1926
N. Thompson	Hull–Sutton–Preston (Holderness)	1926

Fusseys Motors	Hull–Cottingham	1927
Springville Passenger Service	Hull–Hessle	1927
J. C. Holt & Sons	Hull–Newport	1928
Jacksons Motors	Hull–Aldborough–Hornsea	1928

Burn's business led to a further depot, at Withernsea, and the company began to look further north to the Bridlington area, which had not yet – quite – been colonised by a major company. In fact a rapid sequence of takeovers seems to have coincided with, or perhaps been instrumental in, the fixing of territorial boundaries, and events illustrate well the competitive ethics of the 1920s.

The oldest business appears to have been Archer Robinson's Bridlington & District. Robinson, a motor mechanic, began running taxis in about 1905, and up to 1914 ran charabanc trips to such attractions as Flamborough Lighthouse and Scarborough; in the heather season he would go to Whitby and Goathland, 'considered a great adventure in those days'. After 1918 he developed bus services to Flamborough, Driffield, Scarborough and Leeds, together with more local routes. Robinson's fleet, painted green and cream and known as the Green Buses, took over in the mid-1920s a rival Red Bus firm owned by Messrs Trown, Tooth & Twentyman, which had competed directly on most Green Bus routes but departed, because they were so licensed by the Bridlington Council, from a different terminus in Queen Street. When the Red Buses were taken over they were transferred to the Green terminus in Cliff Street whereupon W. H. Atkin commenced running Blue Buses from Queen Street over the same routes. Another operator on the lucrative Bridlington–Scarborough route was Scarborough & District, developed by a Mr Grofton in about 1920, who was in fact the first to be bought out – by United – in 1929. Soon after, Robinson sold too, and for 10 days the business was controlled by United from Scarborough, but by this time the territorial agreement had been made, fixing the East Yorkshire/United boundary between Scarborough and Bridlington. Since most of Robinson's services radiated from Bridlington, East Yorkshire was the beneficiary here, although two United buses remained in Bridlington to work the

Scarborough route. In 1930, a few months later, Atkin sold his Blue Buses, which were again divided between the two companies; even then the story was not quite finished for, as we shall see, there remained in Bridlington Wilson & Hughes' White Bus Company!

Finally, in 1932 the company's strength nearer home was consolidated when Sherwood's Motors of Hornsea was acquired together with two more substantial firms having long histories. The original passenger and goods business of Palframan from Kirk Ella had been purchased in 1885 by the Binnington family, who introduced motor buses in 1910. Eventually this firm was running from Hull to Ferriby and Hornsea and also contributed a cross-country Hessle to Hornsea route which gave a further depot in the latter town. Older still in origin was the Hull City (HC) Motor Works of Beverley Road, Hull, which traded as Kingston Motor Services; although the firm as such came into existence only in 1923, it obtained a service from Hessle to Hull which had first run – horse-drawn of course – in 1867. Kingston also purchased Newington Motor Services (The Red Chara), of Walton Street, Hull, which had taken over the North Eastern Railway's original bus route.

This enterprise in fact had a very early association with BET, when in 1902 the NER examined ways of serving the coastal strip north-east of Beverley and, deciding that a light railway would be uneconomic, was recommended by BET's parliamentary engineer to construct a tramway. After consideration, three buses were ordered, which on 7 September 1903 began a daily service from Beverley to Beeford – so coming a close second to the Great Western's Helston – The Lizard route in the history of railway-owned buses. From the end of the year the service was extended to Driffield on Thursdays, and so continued until 1914; it resumed after the war, running only as far as Brandesburton, but because of losses was handed over to Newington's in 1925.

However, East Yorkshire was not content to grow only by buying out competitors, and in common with other BET companies it took advantage of the growth in long-distance traffic. As early as 1929 an express service was introduced from Scarborough to London via Bridlington and Barnsley, where it connected with a feeder from Hull. In 1931 EYMS became a member of the Yorkshire Services Pool, which was otherwise a consortium of three BET companies (Yorkshire Traction, Yorkshire Woollen District and East Midland) and one Tilling company (West Yorkshire), set up to rationalise their interests in the lucrative traffic from the industrial West Riding to London and the Midlands. East Yorkshire's position was strengthened by the direct purchase in 1933 of two firms, the Hale Garage & Coach Company, and Coachways Ltd, which ran from London to Leeds and Hull, and by the transfer to the pool of Phillipson Stella's London–Scarborough service after the sale of that firm to United in 1934. Obviously the East Riding could not generate the numbers of passengers to be found in such centres as Leeds, Bradford and Sheffield. It is curious, therefore, that EYMS had the status of a major member of the pool, mileage and revenue entitlements being divided as follows:

East Yorkshire 22%
Yorkshire Traction.................... 22%
Yorkshire Woollen District 22%
West Yorkshire........................ 22%
East Midland 12%

The operating problems that this created were solved for many years, certainly into the 1970s, by Hull drivers and coaches literally working tours of duty which kept them away from home for four days. A specimen tour would be:

Day 1 ... Hull–Great North Road–London
Day 2 ... London–Cambridge–Leeds
Day 3 ... Leeds–Cambridge–London
Day 4 ... London–Great North Road–Hull

Co-ordination: EYMS and KHCT to 1945

It is clear that by 1932 East Yorkshire was a force to be reckoned with in Hull. In the wake of the 1930 Road Traffic Act it was necessary to establish a stable service framework and, in so doing, to come to terms with the Corporation; agreements were made between companies and municipalities throughout the country but most, unlike that in Hull, removed or restricted the right of the country operator to carry local passengers in the town area. East Yorkshire's share in Hull local traffic was vital, since there was little other urban business to balance the thin routes of the East Riding Wolds. Fortunately luck was on the company's side in that the pro-tramway policy was under review, and particularly in the appointment of D. P. Morrison as the Corporation's general manager in 1931; Morrison was a bus-minded ex-BET man who had informed the Council on being interviewed that if appointed manager, he must be allowed to manage.

The co-ordination scheme came into effect on 29 July 1934. Administratively it identified three territories: the A area – inner city, the B area – suburbs, including some developing housing areas outside the city boundary, and what has sometimes been called the C area – countryside beyond. All routes entirely within A were to be the Corporation's; each operator would provide 50 per cent of the mileage operated in B, and only East Yorkshire would run beyond into C. Financially, the Corporation kept its revenue from A and put that from B into a pool, which also received East Yorkshire's B revenue and a proportion of that from A, recognising that local passengers would be carried on buses continuing beyond. The total revenue placed in the pool was then redistributed in proportion to the mileage run by each.

Operational changes were also required to make the system work. Where trams ran beyond the A boundary their routes had either to be withdrawn or shortened, leading to five new Corporation bus routes; there were also two other new routes to the Sutton area. These were not, however, the first tram lines to go, since the Pier route had been replaced by buses in 1931, and the Holderness Road line went a year later. Nor was it the first time that operations had been transferred between the partners, since the Corporation had in 1930 and 1932 purchased two routes to Sutton and one to Wawne from the company.

Morrison's counterpart at East Yorkshire in the signing of the agreement was the first fully-fledged general manager, R. T. Ebrey; since Spencer Wills' elevation in 1931 there appears to have been an interregnum with, one feels, Wills looking closely over the shoulders of local management. Ebrey was responsible for the Willebrew ticket system used by East Yorkshire and some other operators, a clumsy device involving cutting out sections of ticket which seemed to be the only way of apportioning fares collected in the A, B and C areas.

The marriage was in a sense consummated by the joint

purchase of Sharpe's Motors of Hedon in 1936, which ran into Hull from that area. In practice, however, the takeover was by the Corporation, which continued to operate the services involved to Hedon, to Paull and to Saltend Works. They were the first to be jointly licensed and the first two were often to be transferred from one partner to the other in order to achieve equal B area mileage apportionment.

So far as vehicles themselves are concerned, for many years nearly all East Yorkshire double-deckers were distinguishable by the strange Gothic shape of the upper deck sides and roof. The reason for this lay in the medieval North Bar at Beverley, which had a nominal height limit of 10ft 9in and through which several important routes passed; the restriction meant that even conventional lowbridge buses, with a sunken gangway upstairs, could not be used. In 1934 a template was made and, from 1935, Leyland Titans with specially shaped roofs to fit the Gothic arch were used. For nearly 30 years all double-deckers, except for a few of the lowbridge type required for bridges in South Cave and Hornsea, were of this pattern. In 1959 AEC brought its Bridgemaster on the market, designed to replace the lowbridge bus with dropped side gangway upstairs by lowering the transmission and floor levels; East Yorkshire hoped that the Bridgemaster would be able to negotiate the Bar but found the fit too tight, and, after the first four, all Bridgemasters, the similar Renowns and a few Daimler Fleetlines incorporated a modified Bar design. Road works completed in 1970 meant that buses no longer needed to pass through the Bar, and the tradition came to an end. It seems a little odd that the Gothic roof was deemed necessary for all East Yorkshire double deckers, when the vast majority were on Hull and Bridlington local routes and only a few actually ran in Beverley; one affected route was that to Leeds, joint with West Yorkshire, which solved the problem by using single-deckers.

D. P. Morrison left the Corporation in 1935. One memorial of his tenancy was the garage and bus station (always called the Coach Station) opened in Ferensway in October. The latter, on an ideal site adjoining Paragon railway station, was also to be used by East Yorkshire and reflected Morrison's conviction that the motor bus would predominate.

In view of this it may seem strange that the tram routes were converted to trolleybuses. In fact the Corporation had already contemplated this when, in 1929, it decided that the density of traffic on the Preston Road route justified their use. Certain that the proposal would be approved by the Council, Guy chassis, bodies and traction poles were ordered in advance. When the Bill to be presented to Parliament was put to a town meeting it was combined with a selection of municipal affairs, many of them outside transport and controversial. A single vote was taken, the motion lost, and all the committee could do was to have the chassis fitted with petrol engines and bus bodies.

Conversion was finally agreed when the co-ordination scheme was in force and the economic situation brighter. In Hull's particular case trolleybuses – or 'trolley vehicles' as they were officially known until 1941 – had special advantages. The straight and wide main roads were highly suitable, they would use corporation-generated electricity, of which it had been agreed to buy £6,000-worth for another 14 years, and, not least, they would not use fuel while waiting at the notorious railway level crossings. There had been seven crossings on tram routes and, for railway safety reasons rather than to reduce disruption, semaphore signals and catch points interlocked with the railway system were used. Nothing was done to remove these bottlenecks until post-war years, when all but one of the important crossings were eliminated. However, traffic in Hull continued to suffer from the lifting bridges to accommodate ships.

In fact, Morrison's successor, J. Lawson, had a strong electrical background, and the committee chairman of the time was an electrician; so the Kingston-upon-Hull Corporation Act of 1936 was fairly predictable. The first route affected was to Chanterlands Avenue, which had been worked by motor buses since 1934, but where electrical equipment was still in position. The buses taken off this route were used to run the next conversion, Newland Avenue, while work was being carried out, and so on, until in 1938 they were transferred permanently to the Hedon Road route; extra trams had been needed here to carry substantial numbers of dockers for whom buses were now available at the appropriate times. Now only the Holderness, Anlaby and Hessle Road trams remained, of which the first was converted by February 1940. Just before this Lawson died suddenly and his successor, G. H. Pulfrey, was not appointed until 1941, when the condition of the remaining tramway was deteriorating rapidly. Sanction for new equipment was, of course, almost impossible to obtain, but conscription and evacuation had reduced the number of passengers so that timetables could be reduced and some of the original trolleybuses delicensed. Thus it was possible to convert Anlaby Road to trolleybuses in 1942, merely by recovering four vehicles loaned to Pontypridd, and, after a mighty struggle, twelve new vehicles were obtained for Hessle Road in July 1945.

It is perhaps not widely appreciated how badly Hull suffered during the war. G. M. O'Connell – an invaluable source – writes: 'The heavy raids of May 1941 were numbered at about 200 in the series of alerts (ie when sirens required to be sounded) which commenced with No 1 on 3 September 1939; . . . Hull's alerts eventually totalled 815! The Germans quite evidently realised that, amongst other things, the bulk of the Russian convoys originated at Hull.' Raids were heaviest in May and July 1941. 'Buses were diverted to side streets to avoid craters and unexploded bombs, short journeys were operated on both buses and trams because of damage and destruction of overhead equipment. Shuttle bus services were instituted, notices of changed services had to be chalked up on notice boards, buildings, and on the pavements'. At the same time much of the overhead line was destroyed together with 38 traction poles. Both the Cottingham Road garage and the headquarters adjoining Ferensway were severely damaged, with a loss of 44 buses; however, the Corporation was able as a result to secure 50 of the elusive utility buses, which then constituted half the diesel fleet.

To minimise the risk of losses . . . all rolling stock not under repair was parked overnight along the main roads on the city outskirts (motor buses in the parks). Instructions were received from higher authority that as it was allegedly possible on moonlight nights to see from the air the lines of vehicles by reason of their predominantly white fronts, they should be repainted: this was expeditiously achieved by overpainting the white areas with blue undercoating. . . . As late as 17 March 1945 12 people were killed and injured outside an East Hull cinema. The remarkable thing about this particular incident was that two fully-laden trolleybuses would have passed each other as the bombs fell but for the fact that *both* drivers had premonitions and did not leave their previous stopping places although signalled to do so by their respective conductors.

By contrast East Yorkshire suffered relatively little. The traffic offices, close to Paragon Station, were bombed and moved permanently to Anlaby Road, where R. T. Ebrey is said to have extinguished one incendiary fire with pint pots of beer. In 1943 he moved to Western Welsh, to be replaced by C. R. H. (Cosmo) Wreathall; this remarkable individual, the son of a BET and EYMS director, continued the fashion for young managers by being appointed at 34 and held the post for a record 31 years until his retirement.

1945 – 1965: East Yorkshire Growth

In the early post-war years EYMS resumed its policy of independent takeovers. All were distant from Hull, the first being Crosby's Motor Services of Hunmanby in 1947; this removed the last private operator into Scarborough from the south. A similar monopoly in Bridlington followed three purchases.

The oldest was the business of R. Williamson and Sons, whose founder had 'given up a seafaring life and commenced keeping a livery stable and running landaus in summer'; by the 1890s he was charging passengers a penny each to be carried in waggonettes from Bridlington Quay to the town centre. His son Reuben and a grandson took over before the sale to EYMS in 1951. Williamson had been a pioneer of motor buses in the area, having introduced in about 1909 a smart French double-decker named *Republic*, but it ran little more than trials; the local hills were too much for it and the horse reigned supreme until after 1918. The last operators of Bridlington local routes, selling in 1955, were John Wilson and Billy Hughes, whose White Bus Service to Flamborough was first licensed by Bridlington Council in the early 1920s. Later, other town routes and local excursions were run, but the fleet never exceeded six vehicles.

Meanwhile another depot had been acquired by the purchase in 1953 of Everingham Bros of Pocklington, with local rural services but also running over the roads to York and Bridlington where EYMS had an interest. The depot was strategically placed on the main Leeds – Hull and Leeds – Bridlington routes and became useful for operating them, but even so a mere nine buses were at Pocklington in 1974 despite an increase in commuter traffic to York. One of the Everingham routes, to Stamford Bridge and York, did not, in fact, pass to East Yorkshire but was sold direct to Bailey's Transport Ltd of Fangfoss, which still runs it over 20 years later. Some of the fleet survived ten years in East Yorkshire service and in 1956 may have been used for the company's first one-man operation, at Pocklington. As at United, one-man operation was a sign of deteriorating finances, but East Yorkshire had never been a wealthy company, placed as it was between the devil of a large rural area and the deep blue sea of a Corporation which could always resort to the rates. In 1957, particularly, no final dividend was paid and an order for new buses was cancelled after a decline in passengers of 10 per cent.

One of the reasons for this drop in traffic may have been the introduction at the time of diesel multiple-unit trains in place of steam on many lines in the North East. As early as 1948 East Yorkshire had competed with one of the Hull commuter lines with its local express from Hornsea, and two years later did likewise from Withernsea. The crisis of 1957 seems to have led to withdrawal of the Hornsea bus route the following year. Nevertheless the bus finally won, for both Hornsea and Withernsea lines were closed in October 1964, and the Hornsea express bus reinstated as 23X, taken from the number of the regular Hornsea – Hull service. Twelve months later the closure of the York – Pocklington – Hull line brought a need for extra journeys which were, similarly on this much longer route, provided as 46X. Unlike the Tyneside limited stops, however, none of these gave regular all-day frequencies. They were always intended for peak traffic and 46X follows a special route through Cottingham for the schoolchildren who provide much of its business.

Although used internally since 1926, East Yorkshire found it possible to survive without publicising their route numbers for a surprisingly long time, until May 1961. When they were finally introduced, some clashed with Corporation numbers and in September 1962 both operators renumbered some routes in the outer suburbs of Hull. At the same time matters were made easier for the travelling public in another way, when the custom of B bus routes giving protection to trolleybuses in the form of a 1d fare surcharge was abolished.

Trolleys to Buses: KHCT, 1945 – 1965

In themselves the trolleybuses were always very successful at Hull. Their arrival in 1937 marked the end of increasing deficits, £27,254 against £1,417 in 1931, and the beginning of surplus, £14,420 in 1937. A maximum fleet of 100 was attained in 1948 when the best route, to Hessle Road, was sometimes run at a 2min frequency. Indeed, the conversion of the busiest A bus route (Greatfield) to trolleys was seriously examined and only discarded when the capital cost was found to be prohibitive. Meanwhile demand was falling off, so that the trolley fleet was down to 89 by 1955, and over the ten years from 1949 to 1959 the trolleys lost 50 per cent of their passengers, while motor buses lost only 12 per cent. Undoubtedly much of the loss could have been attributed to the development of new council estates away from the trolley routes and the consequent shift of population. Allied, too, was the demolition of inner area housing. It was recognised that the density of population in the new estates would not be enough to pay off the capital charges of trolleybus extensions, and accordingly the committee recommended conversion to buses in June 1959. Most people found the idea strange of abandoning a profitable and satisfactory system, and the Council passed the decision back to the committee three times; but in January 1960 a programme was agreed for completion of the changeover by June 1964. The decision proved to be right in that the replacement routes soon needed to be extended into new estates all of which were in area B.

G. H. Pulfrey brought back from holidays spent in America ideas of simplified fare systems, one-man operation and buses with separate entrances and exits. In the early post-war years he concentrated on standardising the fleet, then in the 1950s, when few buses were bought, he experimented with one-man single deckers having centre exits. They were used from 1957 on Sutton routes, but the first one man buses were in fact converted AEC Regals in 1954; when housing development at Bransholme brought increased traffic the routes involved were later turned over to double-deckers again. Most unusually for the time, Pulfrey took the view that with proper equipment one-man operation (omo) of double-deckers was feasible; trolleybus 101, which was exhibited at the Commercial Motor Show in 1952, was the first of 16 to feature a centre exit but also twin staircases – and a periscope, for the driver to watch the upper deck. However, the trades unions and the employers' association did not agree with his views, and his efforts in fitting the last of the 16 with an electronic passenger counter and farebox in 1956 were wasted. Pulfrey did not wish to extend omo on the diesel fleet until buses with a better platform layout were available, and no advances there were made from 1960 until 1966.

The period of extensive fleet replacement in the late 1940s, and the lull which followed in the 1950s, would obviously be repeated when these vehicles themselves became due for retirement. To make matters worse, the trolleybus replacements had to be bought during the next expensive period in the 1960s; finally, the 50 utility buses had had their lives prolonged either by renovating their poor bodywork or fitting superior bodies from pre-war buses, but they too were now at the end of the road. The Corporation therefore took the unusual step of buying 77 respectable second-hand buses from other municipalities, (some came from Newcastle) which could be phased out over a period and so make the renewal programme even. New Leyland Atlanteans were purchased and were adaptable for omo when it became possible.

The Problem Era: 1966 – 1973

On 11 September 1966, grievances which had been simmering at East Yorkshire came suddenly to a head when management put three proposals to the staff. The first was that there should be more split turns, with crews going home between spells on duty. Second, the complicated Willebrew ticket system meant that in Hull there were no omo buses, which elsewhere used the conventional Setright machines; it was now proposed to convert to one-man operation service 46 to Leeds, but to use conductors as far as the Hull boundary. Third it was intended to put an East Yorkshire bus on the co-ordinated service 17, hitherto solely a Corporation route, an apparently innocent proposition which provoked one of the longest strikes in bus history.

Crews declined to work route 17 unless they received wages comparable to those paid to municipal staff. When, by the end of the month, negotiations had brought no progress, it was decided that all depots should strike from 16 October; on 7 November all except Anlaby Road returned to work, since the dispute concerned only the co-ordination area, but on management threatening to discipline the outsiders if they failed to carry local passengers in Hull, the strike widened again to Elloughton, Hornsea and Withernsea. After seven weeks the men returned to work, basically on the management's terms, but it is noticeable that when the Prices and Incomes Board reported later on the bus companies, its proposals included an urban bonus to cater exactly for the Hull situation.

The dispute was notable also for the publication of a booklet, *No Bus Today*, by the Transport & General Workers Union, which revealed that, although pay was particularly bad at the time and affected by a wage freeze, the bonus was a side-issue; above all the men were concerned at the relationship between EYMS and BET. The booklet described the General Manager as a willing tool of BET, lacking local decision-making power, which might otherwise have enabled the bonus to be paid. The booklet continued its tirade against BET:

> 350 Hull men and women are involved in fighting, not a local bus company, but THIS MONSTROUS, SPRAWLING, FACELESS, THOUSAND TENTACLED FINANCIAL OCTOPUS, TO WHOM THESE 350 WORKERS ARE NOTHING AS HUMAN BEINGS, BUT ARE A GREAT MENACE TO THE SATISFACTION OF ITS INSATIABLE APPETITE FOR PROFIT.

This 'octopus' was said also to have a 49 per cent shareholding in the Hull Daily Mail, which spoke out strongly against the strike, but in particular the TGWU ire was directed against the company chairman. Spencer Wills, now Sir John, had joined the BET in 1936. He chaired many bus companies, including BMMO (Midland Red) (the largest) and became managing director of BET in 1946; as the group widened its net, he chaired other companies of which Rediffusion and Wembley Stadium are among the better known.

Wills' special interest in East Yorkshire seems not to have been of any benefit in this affair. It is strange that a dispute apparently over differentials in pay should arise in Hull, where joint running with the Corporation had been taken for granted for 32 years. Perhaps it was precisely that the men felt *they* were taken for granted, as suggested by the complaints of cavalier treatment in industrial relations. In May 1968 the Corporation suffered a ten-day strike, but this was part of a nation-wide municipal protest over wages.

The East Yorkshire dispute provoked comment from Tom Graham, the proprietor of Connor & Graham, which was the only remaining independent in the Holderness area with a daily service into Hull from Kilnsea. Since the closure of the Hornsea and Withernsea railway lines, EYMS provided the only public transport to the area, and Graham suggested that where buses replaced a railway line, at least a minimum peak service should be provided by someone other than the monopoly operator, ie, in this case, himself. The Withernsea town clerk made representations to the traffic commissioners, Members of Parliament and unions, but without success – undoubtedly because they were reluctant to accept the strike-breaking implications.

East Yorkshire's fare-collection problems – conductors in Hull had to carry three separate sets of tickets – were part of the reason for changes in the co-ordination scheme. Equally important, the familiar population movement from city centre to outskirts represented declining traffic in the A area, and growth in the B and C – and therefore increasing deficits for the Corporation. The new agreement, which came into effect on 29 December 1969, simplified the allocation of revenue, so that the Corporation received 70 per cent of the total and East Yorkshire 30 per cent; not now knowing how many passengers on C routes were travelling locally within the B area, East Yorkshire now paid in a proportion of the C revenue. From 1 April 1973 the agreement was changed again, this time with more attention given to mileage.

The 1969 change cleared the way for extensive omo within Hull. East Yorkshire's major problem here was that about three-quarters of the fleet had always been double-deck, and up to 1966 these were half-cab AEC vehicles which could not be one-man operated. On the other hand, the Northern group had many suitable buses still carrying conductors, and in 1972 20 Tynemouth Daimler Fleetlines were sent to Hull in exchange for the last six Renowns, bringing the Beverley Bar design to Percy

Main. As part of the deal East Yorkshire also assigned to Northern ten further Fleetlines still on order; once delivered, these buses soon went to help United solve a similar problem in exchange for Bristol Lodekkas.

The Corporation also lost no time in introducing one-man double-deckers. Pulfrey's successor from 1966, Walter K. Haigh, was well placed to continue his policies from experience as Norman Morton's deputy at Sunderland. Together with the Bell Punch Company he devised the 'Autofare' system by which the passenger pays his fare into a slot and after the driver has checked it, collects his ticket from a separate machine. This brought the average passenger boarding time down to 2·3 seconds and made Hull celebrated in the bus world as the first major organisation to dispense entirely with conductors. After introduction on one A route during 1969, the system spread until all 223 KHCT buses were one-man operated from 13 November 1972. In the last years the few conductors engaged were employed on a temporary basis, and after finding some of them driving, clerical or works jobs, no more than 40 had to be made redundant. Naturally the success of Autofare attracted envy from East Yorkshire staff too, and from March 1974 fare boxes were fitted to company buses in the city; one of the disadvantages of the system is that the passenger has to have the right fare, so there would now be no chance of travellers without change deserting Corporation for company buses.

Like Northern, East Yorkshire was sold by BET and became a subsidiary of the National Bus Company. At least in the East Riding financial crises were no novelty and many routes were tailored to the traffic offering; but for a period in 1970 it looked as if some areas might lose all their buses. Finally the County Council decided on a fairly generous policy of subsidy, which gave aid to all the country routes based at Driffield and Pocklington; only one route from Hull, to Withernsea, was involved. Recent timetables in fact show far fewer service reductions since 1970 than most NBC subsidiaries.

East Yorkshire had already helped out where small independents were finding it no longer worth carrying on. Ideal Motor Services of Market Weighton had once run to Beverley but finally gave up in 1965; East Yorkshire, after unsuccessfully trying substitute services, finally introduced another limited stop service from Pocklington to Hull through the villages affected.

Similarly Gorwood Bros of East Cottingwith wished to give up its service into York in 1967, and it proved possible from February 1968 for EYMS to fit in journeys during the week from Pocklington to serve Gorwood's villages, while Gorwood continued running on Saturdays.

Present and Future

The NBC decree of standardised liveries was a greater hardship to East Yorkshire than, say, United or Northern, where buses were already in a form of red. Not only had buses been painted an attractive dark blue and primrose, with coaches in a lighter blue with Gothic script fleetname, but the roofs were white. There seems to have been a short-lived attempt to preserve an individual touch when it was stated in *Motor Transport* that EYMS intended to preserve the latter feature. C. R. H. Wreathall replied:

Highwayman reported that ... the company wants a white flash painted on the roof of its double-deckers. This is incorrect and there is not, nor has there ever been, any intention to do so.

'Observer' wrote the following week:

I was most surprised to read the letter from Mr. C. R. H. Wreathall ... He should take a look at Bristol VRT number 925 which has been running around the Hull area in just this livery since early December.

Another unusual touch in a major group company was the custom of naming tour coaches after towns in the East Riding with the suffix *Star* – eg *Pocklington Star*. This referred to the company's coach holidays, which were known as Star Tours; the names disappeared as the coaches were painted in National White livery (chapter 4) when responsibility for tours also passed to National Travel.

By coincidence the fleet sizes of the two operators are, within one or two, identical at around 225 vehicles each. The fact that 120 of East Yorkshire's, and, of course, all the Corporation's, are based in Hull shows the overwhelming importance of the city in the public transport of the East Riding (or, now, North Humberside). Will the partnership set up in 1934 continue?

Under the Local Government Act the Hull city boundary was unchanged. In any case the co-ordination scheme took no note of the boundary, which lay inside the B area, and it seems unlikely that local government will be responsible for changing the relationship between the two operators. Within Hull the major preoccupation has been a large council housing scheme at Bransholme, while East Yorkshire is preparing for the opening of the Humber bridge; it is anticipated that services from Hull to Scunthorpe and Grimsby/Cleethorpes will be operated over the bridge jointly with the NBC Lincolnshire company, while a tentative agreement between KHCT and Grimsby/Cleethorpes Transport envisages an all-municipal express service between the two major urban areas of Humberside.

4

LONG-DISTANCE COACHES

Pre-History

The express coach has an important place in the history of the North East generally, and not only in its transport. An area less favoured than others in its climate and job opportunities, remote from the conventional business and holiday centres, and where many incomes were low, created a substantial demand for cheap travel to places with more to offer. Apart from the municipalities most substantial bus organisations, and many small bus firms, have had some interest in long-distance work, resulting in a network of such complexity that it is necessary to devote a separate chapter to this aspect of North East road transport.

It is well-known that the system of stage coaches which, in the early nineteenth century, gave most parts of the country adequate, if infrequent, communication, disappeared very quickly as soon as the vastly greater comfort and speed of a railway was available. A few proprietors struggled on, while the more astute (notably Chaplin and Horne in the South) adjusted to provide feeder services to railheads from areas lacking their own stations; a few of these continued to run in places where branch lines were never built, although they had usually become part of the local bus network by the 1920s. Elsewhere coaches were used temporarily to provide through connections pending the completion of a railway; one ran from Durham to Coxhoe to meet trains to Stockton from 1836, and another, in 1842, from Bishop Auckland to Rainton linking lines then recently opened from Darlington and Gateshead. Otherwise the coach disappeared completely; even where an existing service was not directly replaced by a railway, such as that from York to Middleham, the greater speed of the train over the competitive section would reduce the coach from its previous trunk service to a mere branch at the rural end.

Thus in the early 1920s a road service extending more than, say, 30 miles was virtually unknown. Many have observed that the general strike of 1926 was the beginning of the road express service explosion. It is certainly true that small bus firms mushroomed at the expense of the unionised railways and municipal undertakings at the time, and also that the depression, of which the strike was a symptom, led to a large number of people travelling in search of jobs. However, while this was particularly important in the North East (and also in South Wales, where services to Birmingham and London developed simultaneously) the growth of coach services was nationwide. Equally important was the improved reliability of the bus, and the greater speed and comfort resulting from pneumatic tyres; before 1925 a proprietor would be reckless or optimistic to risk sending a bus a hundred miles from home.

Certainly, long-distance coaches grew from nothing to a major industry in a matter of five years from 1926 to 1931, when the traffic commissioners issued the first express carriage licences. From then on there were relatively few changes until the opening of motorways in the 1960s, when coaches were able to recover some of the ground they had been losing to the private car and railway improvements. Perhaps we may best examine the coach routes of the North East in terms of the broad geographical areas they served.

The Trans-Pennine Routes

Pride of place historically goes to a business which for two reasons should not be here at all; its services have always been licensed as stage carriage rather than express and its headquarters are near Alston in Cumberland. However, Wright Bros of Nenthead has the distinction of running England's highest bus route (at 1,999ft) and being based in the highest village (1,500ft), besides having a depot in Newcastle for its main service to the Lake District.

Even in the heyday of railways, facilities were poor between the East Coast and many of the West Coast resorts, and this was particularly true of the Lakes. In fact the Wright Bros' business began in 1919 as a local affair between Nenthead and Alston, which still exists, mainly as a feeder or running garage journeys for the main route. The fleet grew to half-a-dozen vehicles by 1925 when a 32-seat Guy was purchased with a view to running it between Hexham and Penrith; this was successful mechanically in dealing with the Hartside Pass, rising to 1,889ft, but being based on a lorry chassis its vibration while climbing was none too pleasant! A nearby firm, Ridley of Haltwhistle, began running through from Newcastle to Keswick over the route in the same year, and by taking over this competitor in 1926 the Wrights established themselves. The firm also undertook miners' traffic to Haltwhistle and market day routes to Haltwhistle and Hexham (1926) and to Allendale Town (1928), while from Nenthead the original route was extended back over the watershed into Co Durham to Wearhead and down Weardale to Stanhope. None of these services was very successful, partly for the usual traffic reasons in an upland area but also because of the demands made on vehicles by narrow, hilly roads.

From 1930 the business was stabilised for the years to come, but it also perpetuated a problem for Wrights. In 1928 Northern had begun a seasonal daily tour – ie a daily summer express – from Newcastle to Keswick, running at similar times to Wright, and while there might be enough business for both at weekends this was not always so during the week. Northern received a similar licence to Wright, while the BET Ribble company had a morning departure from Keswick which returned from Newcastle in the afternoon. In winter, from November to Whitsun, Wrights alone ran the service, and between November and Easter only as far as Penrith. At these times most of the traffic was local, with workers to Hexham and Newcastle, or shoppers to Penrith and Hexham, which explains the stage carriage rather than express carriage licence held by the Wrights. During the 1939–45 war this was to their advantage, since express services had to be suspended, including Northern's, and the firm was able to avoid substantial reductions in its live mileage by garaging coaches at Newcastle, so effecting the required savings by eliminating empty runs to Nenthead. The depot was kept, both to accommodate relief coaches overnight and to build up private hire business on Tyneside.

The war was, of course, rapidly followed by the severe winter of 1947, which can have affected few operators more than Wrights. The Alston-Penrith section was suspended since the usual alternative route, via Brampton, was also impassable, and the brothers with their staff turned out to help roadmen cut a way through. Not only did this fail, but Nenthead itself was cut off, and the village's transport men walked to Alston to bring back food in sacks. The road from Alston to Hexham was also closed, which was not to happen again until 1963.

From a 1949 peak of 25 vehicles the business began a decline, for Wrights had problems in all directions. The Tyne Valley colliery traffic was disappearing, Alston and Nenthead, both lead mining communities, were suffering severe population decline, and the market services were losing customers. Of these, only the Hexham Tuesday service survived, while the Stanhope route was cut back to St Johns Chapel and finally withdrawn in 1966, leaving no connections between Alston and Co Durham. In these circumstances it was galling for Wright Bros that on the one worthwhile route a competitor creamed off the traffic during the busiest period; in winter the Penrith section had already been cut back to Alston on three days a week.

An agreement was made between the operators in 1963 based on suggestions from the traffic commissioners. Wright Bros continued to be sole operator from November to Whitsun and as far as short journeys between Alston and Newcastle were concerned. For the summer Keswick service a pool was formed, of which Wrights had a 40 per cent share and Ribble/NGT 60 per cent. In practice Wrights' vehicles have worked the regular weekday runs with Northern appearing at weekends, when there is a journey from Sunderland, and Ribble working the remaining early Saturday departure from Keswick; even so, on a busy Saturday a dozen of the current Wright fleet of 15 vehicles may be needed on the morning departure from Newcastle.

In 1973, at Northern's request, the Keswick service was extended at weekends to Whitehaven, but the traffic anticipated from the extension, which was costly for the Wrights, did not materialise, and for 1974 a link to Bowness and Ambleside was substituted. Before that, in 1971, the winter Sunday service to Penrith had been extended to Keswick following the withdrawal of local Ribble buses which had brought weekend travellers back from the Lakes. At the same time a new local route was introduced from Alston to the village of Garrigill, which had previously had no bus since 1960. Running on alternate Fridays, it is subsidised from the income of a local charity 'to benefit the people of Garrigill'.

A route of similar character to the Newcastle – Keswick service is that from Darlington to Carlisle, mainly following the

A66 road, operated under the name of GNE Motor Services. G. E. Brown was a Leeholme man who, in about 1926, began running into Bishop Auckland from Coundon. Finding the competition too stiff, he formed (with two others) a consortium, the Great North of England Omnibus Co, to run two long-distance routes – Newcastle–Darlington–Richmond–Doncaster, and Darlington–Barnard Castle–Penrith–Carlisle. The Doncaster route was kept only for a short time, and a clash of personalities between Brown, who was strictly temperate and anti-gambling, and the others left Brown in sole charge. He opened a base at Carlisle to operate a return journey from each end daily, using a fleet of Gilfords named after castles along the route.

It is probably not widely known that in the summer of 1933/4 United and Ribble also tried the route, but chose not to continue – thinking it wise to leave it for Brown. The A66 over Stainmore does not have the hairpin bends or extreme altitudes experienced by Wright Bros, the summit being at a mere 1,450ft, but it is similar in its paucity of local traffic, and in winter there is little demand for through travel. Like the Wrights, therefore, GNE needed a stage carriage licence, enabling both local and long-distance passengers to travel and so make the operation worthwhile. The route was, and still is, typical of the old-fashioned country bus; parcels are an important part of the traffic, and together with newspapers are delivered by the driver by being thrown out of the window en route. The tale is told of the unfortunate cyclist who was hit by a newspaper, extra heavy because it contained a monthly supplement, when it was badly aimed at a farm gate. At one time livestock, too, was carried, until a goose, travelling in a sack up to its neck, discovered it had been put next to a parcel of wheat.

Surprisingly there was no direct service from Darlington to the Lakes, and much of GNE's traffic was in passengers transferring at Penrith to Ribble buses, to such an extent that Ribble could not always carry them. GNE therefore introduced in 1959 a summer weekend express to Keswick, superimposed on the existing route as far as Penrith; since there was no competition it was possible to start at Middlesbrough and so tap the larger Teesside market.

A point of difference compared with Wright Bros was that GNE was competing directly with a railway service from

Darlington to Penrith. This line, built principally to carry iron ore eastwards and coal westwards, never carried much passenger traffic and few were upset at its closure in 1962. However, persuaded that there would be increased demand, the firm restored the morning journey from Carlisle which had, by this time, been withdrawn on certain days, and also increased the Keswick frequency. One particular journey, introduced for fell-walkers, carried 25 passengers over nine Saturdays, and by 1970 the timetable was reduced again, leaving the Carlisle departure running only on Saturdays.

G. E. Brown had handed over control to his son Ernest immediately after the war, but by 1971 he was a sick man; the business was sold to a partnership of George Allinson and John Newton, already involved in road haulage. The buiness continues outwardly unchanged, the main occupation of the eight coaches now being at the quality end of the private hire market.

The Lake District was a minor attraction to the people of the North East compared with the holidaymakers' Mecca at Blackpool. The first to tackle this route from Tyneside, both in the summer of 1927, were Northern (running jointly with Ribble) and Robert Bisset. The latter had entered the bus field in the bad days of 1924, when someone else had offered to do his £3 wagon driver's job for £2.10s; he asked his father-in-law, John Patterson, for a loan of £50 to buy a solid-tyred Seddon. Patterson, a canny miner himself, proposed instead a joint enterprise and the two began running over the Scotswood Bridge–Blaydon route. After a season of running to Blackpool in conjunction with R. Gray, Bisset and Patterson joined forces with Graham and Lewins, who also had a bus on the Scotswood–Blaydon route, since coaches went to Blackpool one day and returned the next, so that two were needed. In that year, 1928, the band playing at Blackpool Tower came from Tyneside and, having to take up their duties a week before Easter, asked if the service could start in time to carry them; for the next 20 years Blackpool coaches were to run from Palm Sunday onwards.

The Scotswood buses were discarded in March 1930 when the Blaydon A proprietors (chapter 5) sold out, but Bisset argued that as his Blackpool coach was completely separate it should not be included in the sale. He and Robert Graham duly received their express licence from the Commissioners in 1932, but not before Blackpool Corporation had objected to the use of their terminus in the town. Speaking for the operators was T. H. Campbell Wardlaw, later the uncrowned king of transport lawyers and then beginning his career. The Corporation, he said, was spending thousands on publicity to attract people to Blackpool; here was a man seeking to bring them in, and the same Corporation was trying to keep him out! The Bisset/Graham service needed a corporate image and, since the next Bisset coach was delivered in yellow, 'Primrose Coaches' was chosen. The two businesses remained, as they still are, entirely separate, and indeed Graham Bros coaches are not primrose in colour at all, but beige and cream.

When express services were curtailed by the second world war, the partners had to find other work and Bisset provided buses on contract to United to run to the Royal Ordnance Factory at Aycliffe. As soon as the Blackpool service could be started again, Primrose anticipated the post-war travel boom in applying to run all the year round. At this time Northern and Ribble ran from Whitsun until the end of September, while Primrose's season was from Palm Sunday until the end of the Blackpool Illuminations, which had gradually become later. In fact a similar application had been made to the commissioners before 1939, but had been refused for fear of coaches becoming snowed up in the Pennines; this was curious since the route ran via Bishop Auckland, Bowes, and Kirkby Stephen, using Stainmore Pass, where both GNE and the London–Glasgow service were licensed to run all year, not to mention Wright Bros' still more arduous route. The post-war application was initially adjourned, because counsel for Northern, which objected, was prevented from travelling into Newcastle across the river from Whickham by snow; when the case was heard later, before a new chairman of the commissioners, and the Pennine snowdrifts were once more brought up, Robert Bisset remarked drily that he knew a man who couldn't even get from Whickham to Newcastle when it snowed.

A joint operation scheme now had to be evolved for the winter period when nobody had been running. Thus from 1 November to Palm Sunday Primrose and the BET companies were to operate 50 per cent each, creating an unusual pattern over the year as follows:

		Ex Newcastle	Ex Blackpool
	Day 1	Graham	Northern
1 November–	Day 2	Northern	Graham
mid	Day 3	Bisset	Northern
January	Day 4	Northern	Bisset
	Day 1	Graham	Northern etc.
Mid January	Day 1	Graham	Ribble
–Saturday	Day 2	Ribble	Graham
before Palm	Day 3	Bisset	Ribble
Sunday	Day 4	Ribble	Bisset
	Day 1	Graham	Ribble etc.
Palm Sunday	Day 1	Bisset	Graham
–Friday	Day 2	Graham	Bisset
before	Day 1	Bisset	Graham etc.
Whitsun			
Whit Saturday	Day 1	Graham	Bisset
–31 October		Ribble	Northern
	Day 2	Bisset	Graham
		Northern	Ribble
	Day 1	Graham	Bisset
		Ribble	Northern etc.

Clearly a major problem was the low utilisation of coaches arising from the two-day circuit; there was little point in increasing the service during the week, but a late departure from each end at weekends made sense. When this was authorised in 1963 another commissioner, J. A. T. Hanlon, granted it subject to the strange condition that the Primrose Friday evening journey should not be advertised in any way. The restriction remained until Northern and Ribble proposed a Newcastle–Southport express in 1969, when Primrose agreed not to object provided that it could run its own service, and that the advertising prohibition be withdrawn.

Apart from this, efforts in the 1960s were mainly directed to improving the attractiveness of the main route. Primrose developed feeder services from the Tyneside hinterland, balancing the Northern/Ribble summer operation which ran from South Shields, and the opening of the M6 motorway in Lancashire permitted the inclusion of Morecambe as an additional major destination on the route from 1974.

At the outbreak of the second world war Graham Bros and Bisset each had three coaches, which increased to 14 and 10 respectively. While Robert Graham continued to control his business, which became more involved in workers' contracts, Bisset died in 1960. From then on R. & M. Bisset Ltd had the distinction of possibly being the only coach firm of any size managed entirely by women – Robert's widow Margaret and daughters Rita Ebdon (Secretary) and Joyce Grant. By contrast, no contract work is undertaken and, most unusually in a private coach firm, only full-time drivers are employed.

The Tyneside–Blackpool operators, of course, have not provided the only facilities from the North East, although they have given the only daily service. Earliest of all was the route commenced by Fred Scott of Darlington in 1923. Once a Darlington Tramways conductor, Scott used a grey horse to deliver groceries before buying, in about 1921, a motor wagon which could be converted into a passenger vehicle at weekends, hence the name 'Scott's Greys'. The Blackpool service originally ran on three days a week in summer (as it still does), using the more southerly Richmond–Hawes–Ribblehead route, and changed little until Scott's death in 1952. The business was then sold to the Hunter family, who were more interested in the haulage activities which Scott had also undertaken. However, they saw the value of developing the coach business and in fact dabbled in local bus work from 1954 to 1957, when they acquired the routes to Darlington of Croft Motor Services and Voy of Newton Aycliffe, which also had a Blackpool licence. This was retained as a useful and growing addition when United took over the local routes, since when the firm has grown by concentrating on contract work and wide-ranging excursions, some of which also originated with Voy. The coach fleet, which grew from 11 in 1964 to 16 a decade later, still carries Scott's fleetname on grey/dark blue with his slogan 'Glorious Runs and Safe Returns'.

It would be surprising if United did not have an interest in Blackpool traffic, but in fact it was relatively late into this market and expanded its share mainly by takeovers. Jointly with Ribble it introduced a daily summer service from Middlesbrough in 1934, substantially following Scott's route but running via Kendal rather than Ribblehead; it also ran from Middlesbrough on five days over the longer and most southerly route of all, through Harrogate, Skipton and Preston. However, in 1929, Wilkinson's (chapter 1) had started running to Blackpool on three days a week in summer, beginning in Trimdon and making a lengthy anti-clockwise tour of Durham mining villages; the beauty of this was that at Spennymoor, whence it followed the Primrose/Northern route, it happened to connect with the Wilkinson bus timing from Stockton, and at holiday times large numbers of duplicates would run from Stockton to Spennymoor, passing through villages not on the coach route, and then continue to Blackpool. It was recognised by United that Wilkinson, despite having no licence to carry from Stockton to Blackpool, in fact carried more traffic than they did themselves.

Darlington Triumph (chapter 1) also had a summer Saturday licence beginning at Sunderland and then passing through many of the same villages as Wilkinson before following the same route. With the rest of David Todd's activities this passed through Durham District to United, permitting a tidying-up exercise in 1969. Since Northern had a Sunderland leg on its long-established service, the Wearside DDS traffic was transferred, while a new pattern was worked out for the mining villages and Teesside, where United now had a Blackpool monopoly apart from a summer Saturday service of Saltburn Motor Services (chapter 6).

Last in this section are the interurban routes known sometimes as the 'Tyne–Tees–Mersey', or, more often, simply as the 'Limited Stop'. They began in August 1927, when coaches began running four times daily between Newcastle and Leeds; probably this was the Leeds & Newcastle Omnibus Co of Northallerton, through which town the service passed, and interestingly the journey took $3\frac{1}{2}$ hours, the same as in 1976. It must have been successful since competition was provided by Bunting and Taylor two months later and Star Motor Services of Newcastle, whose innovation was an overnight coach running through to Liverpool, returning the next night. Inevitably Northern came on the scene in May 1928 with a non-stop Newcastle–Liverpool day service, but a year later an important change was made. Three other group companies, West Yorkshire, North Western and Yorkshire Woollen District, formed a pool with Northern, to provide a two-hourly frequency to Manchester and after a further two months East Yorkshire too became a member, branching eastwards at Leeds to run from Manchester to Hull or Bridlington. The western end of the trunk route took on its final form when, after Liverpool was once more made the terminus, an hourly service between Liverpool and Manchester was incorporated; this was run by North Western, together with Lancashire United which thus became, probably in 1931, the only independent company ever to belong to the Northern pool.

East Yorkshire's contribution seems not to have been very successful as it was withdrawn in 1934. However, the long Leeds–York–Hull and Leeds–York–Bridlington routes, which had been running jointly with West Yorkshire since 1929 and 1930, gave regular connections at Leeds. Meanwhile things were happening at the northern end. Railway purchases in 1929 had included James Frazer's Redwing Motor Services of Redcar, running locally and to Leeds, and in 1933 the business passed to United, which a year earlier began working between Middlesbrough and Leeds jointly with West Yorkshire. Purchase by the pool of the original Leeds and Newcastle company, also by then operating from Leeds to Middlesbrough and Sunderland, removed the last competitor, and also strengthened United's status as the territorial company on Teesside. In October 1934, therefore, the pool members became six once more, as follows (with post-1942 groupings):

Northern General	BET
United Automobile	Tilling
West Yorkshire	Tilling
Yorkshire Woollen District	BET
North Western	BET
Lancashire United	Independent

The timetable was reorganised to run hourly from Liverpool, alternately to Newcastle or Middlesbrough. In later years the Middlesbrough leg was separated and run as a connecting service from Leeds by West Yorkshire and United; most unusually with large companies, it also acted as a local bus over the Ripon–Stockton section, and in practice United's regular pool activity has been confined to this route.

Obtaining good utilisation demanded a complex operating pattern, with coaches regularly staying overnight in depots away from home, and their crews exchanging en route (always at Leeds and Manchester, and sometimes elsewhere); for example the first morning departure from Newcastle might be a Lancashire United coach with a Northern crew. Passing through a series of industrial towns, rather than being substantially point to point, the limited stop service always had a low average speed. For the summer of 1967 an attempt was made to improve matters by running a luxury express service, stopping only at the principal towns, but it was not well patronised, perhaps because passengers were required to book in advance, in contrast to a tradition of pay-on-the-bus. A similar reduction in time on the through Newcastle journeys was achieved by using the M62 motorway from its opening in 1971.

The luxury express title used in 1967 indicates the weaknesses of the established services, which seem to have been a poor relation among long-distance services. Over the years the frequency was reduced to two-hourly (Liverpool–Leeds) and thrice daily (Leeds–Newcastle), with extra journeys at summer weekends, and part at least of the decline must be attributed to the assorted and inferior rolling stock that has customarily been used; nor did the companies find it easy to cater for the unpredictable levels of traffic that resulted from pay-on-the-bus.

Although connecting industrial areas, the limited stop has been used overwhelmingly by holidaymakers.

London

No other destination attracted as much interest or competition as the capital. The pioneers in 1926 were the Orange brothers of Bedlington, followed closely by Robert Armstrong of Ebchester; his 'Majestic Saloon Coaches' at first left Newcastle for London on Sundays, coming back on Fridays, then ran on the alternate days when Orange did not, and by August 1927 both were running every day. At some stage, after 1928, both extended their routes north to Edinburgh and Glasgow, and, as one might expect of operators based outside the Tyneside conurbation they built up connections from the outlying mining districts.

Others soon jumped on the bandwagon. 'North Road Coach Services', introduced in 1927 by a Mr Friar of Blaydon, was purchased by the London firm still operating as Glenton Tours to become Glenton Friars (Road Coaches) Ltd. The Chester-le-Street business 'Cestrian' which ran from Sunderland to London via York from 1929, made an early experiment with double-deckers for long-distance work, and at one time also served Glasgow; F. Taylor of Middlesbrough began a 'Blue Band' service to London from Sunderland via Teesside and York, sometimes following the coast to Scarborough.

One of the factors which encouraged these operators was the overdue increase in the speed limit for heavy motor cars in 1928 from 12 mph to 20mph. It is clear that even this was unrealistic, for the chief constable of the North Riding in November staged a campaign to catch speeding coach drivers. Blue Band drivers seem to have made more appearances than most:

> A bus being driven by Watts on the North Road on 14 November had been followed from York City boundary to Skelton Springs, a distance of three miles, by Superintendent Welford and Sergeant Craven in a motor car and the bus averaged 37¼mph. The bus went at 42mph at one place and round a dangerous corner at 32mph. When stopped Watts said 'I have no speedometer on. I am governed at 40. The firm should alter the timetable. We leave York at 5.30 and arrive at Middlesbrough at 7.30. It is the driver who has to suffer'.

Some of the North-East operators used the terminal and booking facilities of the Central London Road Transport Station near Tottenham Court Road. Frank Lyne, who controlled the station, purchased Cestrian and Blue Band to form National Coachways Ltd in close association with Glenton Friars. While National, operating on the Middlesbrough/Sunderland route, was noted for its timekeeping – 'it was jokingly put around that the town clocks of Middlesbrough set their time by the regularity of National passing through' – Glenton Friars on the Great North Road offered new heights of luxury. Nine Daimlers with Hoyle bodies of the newly-fashionable 'observation coach' style, with three steps up to a raised rear portion, were introduced to potential customers in London by touring the streets.

> While passers-by, and booking agents and staff, were invited to inspect the coaches, a kilted piper marched to and fro. The sound of bagpipes attracted a large crowd and hundreds of leaflet timetables were distributed.

Operators were now working flat out, sending their coaches in one direction by day and returning them by night; the traffic manager of National remarked that one engine had not been cold for nine days. With so much traffic being carried on overnight services, the Express Omnibus Co (Reliance) of Darlington in December 1928 introduced sleeper coaches on Guy six-wheel chassis, incorporating 12 bunks with reading lights, occasional chairs, a shaving mirror and a light refreshment buffet; the fare charged was 32s (£1.60) single or 58s (£2.90) return compared with the others' fare of £1 single. A *Northern Echo* reporter tried the service and informed readers:

> Darlington left to the rear, I settled down for the night, and a few hours and many scores of miles later a voice in the berth above awoke me ... The one disturbing incident was when a member of the party dropped his collar stud.

Against this, Armstrong informed his customers:

> The Majestic Coaches are the latest type of long-distance saloons.
> Electrically heated, arm chair seating.
> Everything for your comfort.
> In the interest of cleanliness and hygiene these cars
> are not fitted with lavatory accommodation.
> The Night Buses are fitted with special reclining seats.

The proprietor of Express was A. A. Speke, also a director of the better-known Harvey group – Varsity Express (London to Oxford and Cambridge) and Varsity Coaches (London to Bournemouth and Poole). While the Darlington local bus routes were sold to the LNER and passed to United, nothing more was heard of the sleeper coach venture and we must presume that it failed.

So 1930 came, and neither Northern nor United had a London service. Without current operations, no licence would be obtained and United lost no time in making offers to the established businesses. The first to sell, in April 1932, were Glenton Friars and National, followed by Majestic's 20 coaches in August, though not before Armstrong had considered a merger with Orange. That firm in fact sold to the Tilling Group, rather than United, in September 1934, but its fleet of 29, less five which went to Scottish Motor Traction, was put under United's wing, and here there is an intriguing mystery. E. B.

Hutchinson had left United after the sale to Tilling in 1929, but in some way he was involved in the Orange deal; possibly he was an intermediary between buyer and seller, or he may have become financially involved in Orange himself in the last months.

Orange Bros had a far greater influence on United than the other coaching acquisitions. It was normal to keep the previous operators' trading name and licences, mainly to operate as many coaches as possible when the commissioners were trying to reduce duplication; while most disappeared by 1935 under the commissioners' pressure, the Orange name survived until the early 1950s, when coaches named 'Orange/United' still ran on the Great North Road. Not only this, but United continued to use the olive green and cream livery, and Orange's distinctive style of fleetname, on its own coaches for 40 years.

In 1933 County Motors, also a local operator in Northumberland, had sold out. A month after Orange, Phillipson Stella Motor Services – serving the Great North Road and running between London and Scarborough – followed suit and there was now only one competitor left. This was J. Charlton & Sons of Red House Garage, Hebburn, who claimed to be 'The original Sunderland–London service'; in fact there were two routes to London from the Tyneside towns, one mainly via the Great North Road and the other via Teesside and York. Charlton finally sold in March 1936, giving United a monopoly of coaches from Tyneside and Teesside to London, a position which was most unusual in the North East. The pattern of services settled down to day and night journeys on each of the traditional Great North Road and Hartlepool–Teesside–York routes. It did not change radically until the building of the M1 motorway and improvement of the A1 in the 1960s, when alternative fast and slow routes were introduced; north of Darlington coaches followed varying routes to give a direct service to most of the Durham mining area.

The Midlands, and Others

Many of the passengers travelling from Tyneside to London in the late 1920s must have been victims of the depression looking for new jobs. While many unemployed Welsh miners made for London, the new Slough trading estate, or Oxford's motor works, those from the North East often chose the Midlands, the only other area offering reasonable employment prospects.

The Fawdon Bus Company (Reed and Turnbull) began a Newcastle–Coventry service in July 1928 after its Newcastle local operations had come under pressure from the Corporation (chapter 5), and, after that side was sold in July 1930, Fawdon continued a further three years before being bought by Northern on behalf of the Northern pool. At this time the service followed the Great North Road south to Wetherby, then passing through Leeds, Sheffield, Derby and Birmingham, so that from Leeds it followed exactly the Yorkshire–Birmingham route of the Yorkshire services pool; since it was half in the territory of the Northern pool (north of Leeds) and the Yorkshire pool (south of Leeds), the route was made joint between all nine members of the two pools. For many years, the Fawdon Bus Co remained in legal existence as holder of the licence, while owning no coaches. Overwhelmingly they were to be supplied by the Yorkshire Woollen District Company, which was a member of both pools and conveniently in the middle of the route, while Northern provided extras needed at the Newcastle end. Later the service, to be known as the 'Ten Cities', was diverted via Harrogate rather than Wetherby, making its northern half identical to the limited stop and, incidentally, an ideal medium for the distribution of West Yorkshire publicity to other companies! The basic once-daily operation was supplemented by a feeder from Halifax and Huddersfield meeting the southbound coach at Barnsley, and by summer weekend overnight journeys.

We can see the social context of these operations better in the case of Hall Bros. It will be remembered that G. E. Brown abandoned his Newcastle–Doncaster express, whereupon the Hall brothers, Edward and John Hubert, took it on in 1930 with an extension south to Nottingham. Initially it did not do well, but the brothers saw the possibilities of a coach service to cater for the hundreds of workers going south with their families. Before long the service was running to Leicester and then to Coventry, while the northern terminus, and Hall Bros headquarters, became South Shields. Interestingly the Red House Garage at Hebburn, home in the early 1930s of Charlton's Blue Safety Coaches, was latterly owned by Edward Hall and used for garaging his fleet; at Coventry, coaches were

103

serviced at another Red House Garage which also ran coaches but had no connection whatever with Hall!

Carrying emigrants from Tyneside was all very well, but of course it was largely a one-way traffic. After the depression ended there were thousands of families living in the Midlands with relatives and friends in the North East, which meant that traffic remained fairly brisk and there was little falling-off of traffic as the drift southward was checked. Moreover the pattern of the 1930s was repeated after the second world war when the closure of Durham pits began and many families chose to move to the East Midlands coalfield with its more modern, long-life collieries, especially, it appears, around Mansfield which was on Hall Bros' route. Here was an advantage which balanced the Ten Cities control of traffic to Birmingham, and it led to an all-year-round and overnight service from 1953; services were publicised by leaflets asking 'Are ye gannin' hame, hinnie?' Also the route followed the Great North Road direct from Newcastle, distant from many of the towns where passengers lived. In 1962 the company started a new route which, between Darlington and South Shields, served Stockton, Hartlepool and Sunderland.

Edward Hall was ready to retire in 1967, and in August sold the business to Barton Transport of Nottingham, one of the big three independents then remaining; 36 coaches in black, ivory and red, none more than three years old, were soon painted in the Barton red, cream and brown. Hall Bros' only licence apart from the Midlands service was for race excursions, but Barton continues to collect a good deal of Tyneside private hire work.

Some other express routes from the North East have a long history, but all were seasonal; a couple of examples will suffice. The nearest United came to the gimmicks of Express and Glenton Friars on the London route was the Yorkshire Coast Express, a daily summer service from Newcastle to Scarborough introduced in 1928. In the 1930s conductors on this route sold refreshments, while passengers could buy cigarettes from machines; observation coaches were used, which were probably the Glenton Friars vehicles. United may have had its East Anglian origins in mind when, in 1932, another daily service began to Lowestoft, jointly with the offspring Eastern Counties company. This ran through Peterborough, Norwich and Great Yarmouth and was designed largely to cater for Geordies holidaying in East Anglia.

The Package Deal and Bee-Line

While the operations so far dealt with offered variety in their destinations, they essentially catered for a part of their passengers' journeys rather than the whole of them. We should remember, too, that besides these businesses there were many either without licences or licences only for excursions and tours. One such firm, Bee-Line Roadways, concentrated on the complete package, in this case the holiday business.

In 1922 Roy Braithwaite took a party from Stockton by train and boat to Calais on a visit to the first world war battlefields; this was the beginning of a tour business which duly received licences after 1930, but Braithwaite never owned a coach. Initially he hired them from United, but from about 1934 he used Bee-Line Safety Coaches, whose proprietor John Wilson had been manager of P. S. Blumers, a company running between Stockton and Hartlepool which had been taken over by United. Braithwaite, who had been wounded in the 1914–18 war, found increasing difficulty in managing his business, although this did not prevent the setting-up of a haulage business, which was nationalised in 1949. At the outbreak of the second world war Braithwaite's Tours became a subsidiary of Bee-Line; he died in 1944. After the war Wilson built up a programme of inclusive tours and obtained a foothold in Middlesbrough by purchasing the very old Bluebird Coaches firm in the town; he also obtained Continental tours which were run under the name 'Pegasus' but they were re-sold to Northern General. In 1959 Bee-Line thus had a fleet of 22, which was largely involved in contract work.

The next major development was the purchase of Hardwick's Tours in 1963, also of Middlesbrough and owned by Roy Hardwick, who had, again, begun with battlefield tours but after the 1939–45 war. Hardwick had continental licences and had sold because of ill-health, but recovered after a year; he and Wilson put their heads together with their accountant, Trevor Barker, and decided to make Bee-Line Roadways the subsidiary of a new company, Gold Case Travel, which would develop travel agencies selling both its own and other operators' holidays. These agencies came to total 18 in the North East, one in every major town, and created two problems for the coach operating side, first the difficulty under the licensing system of giving each of those towns facilities equal to those on Teesside, and second that of getting passengers booked on other operators' package tours to the airports in the south where they usually started. One firm in particular, Clarkson, included the North East in its catchment area for the first time in 1969 and 'arranged' that Gold Case should convey passengers to Luton Airport through its subsidiary. Perhaps on reflection Bee-Line tried to do too much too quickly; at any rate its dealings in the Traffic Courts in the next three years led to a quarrel on an unprecedented scale with United and the commissioners. The principal actors in the drama were Barker, now managing director since Wilson's retirement in 1969, T. H. Campbell Wardlaw, advocate and director, and J. A. T. Hanlon, chairman of the commissioners.

In some early cases where, against opposition from United, Bee-Line sought to increase picking-up facilities on its tours, Campbell Wardlaw came to the conclusion that their treatment was less than fair; it appeared that passengers travelling cheaply (ie by Bee-Line) were expected to suffer greater inconvenience than those who travelled with higher priced operators (ie United). Bee-Line, therefore, should not be allowed to make its passengers' lives easier, which 'was a monstrous argument and showed an outrageous attitude on the part of the commissioners'. Later, when Bee-Line applied to carry tour passengers to Teesside Airport, the commissioners held there was 'no case to answer', and an application to pick up tour passengers at Billingham was granted – on Sundays only. Campbell Wardlaw considered this 'an anachronism without practical justification and with all the appearance of senseless red tape'. Bee-Line, by judicious use of the local press, was certainly encouraging the public of Teesside in this view.

Having effectively lost all these cases, Bee-Line naturally felt a grievance, but they paled into insignificance beside the Luton affair. Originally, in 1970, Barker sought to carry Clarkson clients from Hartlepool to Luton Airport, which lay a couple of miles from United's motorway route to London. The case was adjourned, for Bee-Line to find when it eventually came up that an identical application by United was granted. Not only was an appeal made to the minister as might be expected, but a High Court order was sought to quash the decision on grounds that the proceedings had been conducted in a manner contrary to natural justice.

In the High Court, Bee-Line alleged that 'in adjourning the hearing, the commissioners were descending from their judicial bench into the arena and, in effect, putting their own contender into the field. From then on it was a foregone conclusion that Bee-Line would fail if United chose to apply for a licence.' The order was refused, but an appeal was won. Bee-Line then proceeded, in February 1972, to apply to carry anyone, not only Clarkson passengers, from Newcastle to Luton. Apparently disregarding the ministry inspector's sympathy in the previous case, the commissioners refused the licence through disapproval of Gold Case's 'private arrangements' with Clarkson, and for good measure criticised Clarkson's failure to use the licence granted to United. 'This confirms that Clarkson's interest in how their passengers get to Luton is of no interest (sic) to them except under some commercial agreement between them and Gold Case Travel'.

Bee-Line naturally appealed against this decision too. The minister shared the unease of the inspector 'that the commissioners should have referred to the commercial policies of Clarksons and their business associates in such derogatory terms. Operators are in his view entitled to a dispassionate appraisal of their legitimate efforts to advance their business interests.' He ordered the commissioners to grant the licence, with the result that both rivals would provide the service jointly. Possibly this, and possibly the emergence of a third ambitious operator on Teesside, closed the ranks and the quarrel came to an end. At various times Bee-Line had itself made unkind remarks about United, for example that they were amateurs in coach tours while Bee-Line were professionals. Certainly there was evidence of preferential treatment, when after the Tilling–BET merger, United and Northern sought to combine their tour licences and so double the availability of tours from each area. This passed the commissioners without a murmur; a similar application from Bee-Line would doubtless have been refused.

Litigation had not prevented Gold Case from expansion elsewhere. The group had purchased three hotels, of which two were sold in 1971 in order to purchase Salopia Saloon Coaches, based in Whitchurch with a complementary extended tour business. This brought the fleet to 140, but no coaches were involved in the acquisition, soon after, of the small Ernie

Harkness firm in Penrith. Barker was also developing foreign contacts to carry tourists visiting England, but was hindered by not having a base in the South, and the opportunity was taken in 1973 to buy the London firm of Charles W. Banfield. In turn Bee-Line became part of the much larger Ellerman group, with Trevor Barker continuing as chairman. A total of 180 coaches established Bee-Line among the major independents in Britain, but it can be seen that this is only a part of a total leisure activity. In view of the financial difficulties which, from 1973, beset tour operators in general, and Clarkson in particular, Gold Case was probably well advised to put its eggs in a good many baskets.

Today: National Travel

The National Bus Company obtained from Tilling and BET the vast majority of all-year-round express services. In some parts of the country this amounted to a monopoly and while there are more private operators than usual in the North East, NBC came to have at least a finger in all the important pies.

Generally, coach services had not lost passengers in the way that local buses had, which must be attributed partly to their ability to provide village to village services after Dr Richard Beeching (then chairman of British Railways) largely reduced railways to an Inter-City network. However, it was felt that there was wide-spread public ignorance of services, because they were controlled by local companies who could not sell them adequately in other parts of the country. Often, too, one company would be prevented from expanding its services because a local company elsewhere feared loss of its own traffic. Again, for historical reasons, as in the case of East Yorkshire, a route might be provided by other than the geographically most logical company.

The answer to this was to set up, in 1972, a series of regional companies under the name of National Travel which would develop the coach network as necessary and, in the long run, arrange for coaches to be provided as most convenient. To increase public awareness, all NBC coaches were to be painted similarly in white with a large 'National' fleetname, although some coaches still carried bus company fleetnames but were otherwise identical in white livery.

One administrative effect was the abolition of the Northern and Yorkshire pools. This had little effect on operations, although a 1974 reorganisation in the North West led to Ribble taking over limited stop work from Lancashire United, so ending independent representation on the route. The name of a defunct BET company in the West Riding, Hebble, was adopted for coaches in the area, which replaced YWD on the pool routes. The previously unthinkable also happened when Northern coaches appeared on United's London service.

There was, of course, a particularly strong tradition of coaching among the North-Eastern companies, and much of the new activity under National Travel originated with United and Northern. Already motorways were being used to connect Tyneside with the extensive Associated Motorways network at Cheltenham and to continue at weekends to Paignton; from 1974 East Yorkshire also began running to Cheltenham by extending the old Yorkshire pool service from Hull to Birmingham. Another 1974 innovation, an enterprising service from Teesside and Tyneside to Belfast via Stranraer and Larne, was in fact planned by United. In the same year railway objections temporarily prevented the East Yorkshire Hull–Newcastle route from being extended to Edinburgh and Glasgow. Another interesting new route was introduced in 1973, from Newcastle to Pwllheli, which involved a Northern and a Crosville coach leaving each end simultaneously on summer Saturdays; initially the drivers exchanged en route and on alternate weeks each company had use of the other's coach for a week before returning.

5

TYNE & WEAR

Trams

If, in the late nineteenth century, Britain was the workshop of the world, its north-east corner was Britain's workshop. Newcastle, the existing regional capital, astride the Great North Road and at the lowest bridging point on the Tyne, became, with Gateshead on the opposite bank, the centre of its industry and commerce. Much of the prosperity came from engineering and shipbuilding, which was concentrated along both banks of the Tyne in a linear conurbation ending at North and South Shields; favourable conditions existed also at Sunderland, with deep water at the mouth of the Wear, while both rivers were natural choices for the transport of Durham coal. These various factors combined to bring unprecedented growth to the area from 1870 onwards and so, as the towns increased in population, a demand for cheap local transport.

In each case horse tramways were used, constructed by the Corporation and, since it was then thought that local authorities lacked legal powers to operate themselves, leased to outside companies. First (in 1878) and largest was the Newcastle system, with 40 cars running over 12 route miles, including a three-mile track to the then satellite town of Gosforth. Similarly in the next year a smaller system began under the auspices of the Sunderland Tramways Company. This undertaking experimented with steam trams and found it necessary to use double-deck cars on the sea-front route to Roker, where on sunny days it experienced competition from improvised horse buses. Finally, population increase and the authorisation of a tramway in North Shields led to public pressure for such a facility on the opposite bank. South Shields Corporation was initially persuaded by its lessee to construct the tramway to a narrower gauge than that authorised, apparently to prevent through operation across the Tyne Dock frontier from Jarrow, where a standard-gauge tramway was also proposed. In 1883 the South Shields Tramways Company began business, but disappeared abruptly and mysteriously in 1886, probably due to a long-term inability to show a profit. It was succeeded by a new lessee, the South Shields Tramways and Carriage Company, sponsored by the Newcastle operator. Having had the foresight to secure a lower rental than its predecessor, it was far more profitable and also introduced four miles of bus routes of which the longest, to Harton, was also successful; however, this very success led to a takeover in 1899 by BET.

Meanwhile, the town was growing at a phenomenal rate, the population almost doubling between 1880 and 1900, which made the original system of five route miles inadequate. After its experience with the first lessees, South Shields Corporation was now determined to operate an electrified network itself and secured assent for two phases of expansion, meanwhile granting BET only a five-year lease. When it was ready to go ahead, it followed that BET must be dislodged from the existing route and a year's notice was served from February 1905. The new system began operation in June 1906, followed by various additions to form, a year later, a figure-of-eight between the town and Tyne Dock, plus a branch to the Pier Head. A through service by BET's Jarrow trams to the Pier Head began in 1908, with South Shields retaining all revenue above a given figure, but when the Corporation sought to lower this threshold in 1911 the arrangement ceased.

A similar process took place in the neighbouring towns. An Act of 1899 gave Newcastle Corporation power to electrify, extend, and take over its tramways; in the event the lessee ceased operating rather than continue while reconstruction was going on, and for eight months in 1901 no service was provided at all. This proved a great incentive to hurry the work, which was completed by the end of the year with 14 miles of track; extensions up to 1914 increased this mileage to 63 and included a long route westwards outside the city to Throckley, then mainly a rural area. The Sunderland company, having failed in an attempt to reduce its rental, did not resist an electrification-and-extension proposal in about 1897. After refusing the inevitable advance from BET, the Corporation took over in March 1900 and opened the electrified network, slightly different from that worked by horses, in August.

All three systems were extended over the next 20 years. One of Newcastle's more remarkable lines was that to Gosforth, which continued to the racecourse at Gosforth Park. From 1924 this was linked with the West Moor route by a light railway through the Park, which boasted a station adjoining the grandstand. Hearse recalls, 'In the summer months open-top cars ran an 11-mile circular service from Pilgrim Street to Gosforth Park, returning via Benton and Byker Bridge. On at least one summer Saturday every season children were able to ride on any car in Newcastle for $\frac{1}{2}$d the full distance; the trams were packed with happy children and the Park Circle was naturally very popular.' In the same period (chapter 2) the connection was made with the Gateshead system across the High Level and Tyne bridges.

A new line was built from South Shields to Cleadon, the site of extensive council housing development after 1920, and as it now came within striking distance of the Wearside tracks discussions took place once more on a through tramway, but Sunderland proposed a more easterly route through Whitburn, and no more came of it. At the opposite end, the Jarrow through service recommenced in 1922, this time operated by both parties, but by 1925 South Shields Corporation was complaining of losses on the route and gave the Jarrow company 12 months notice to cease in 1927. At this stage the whole system was losing money through the effect of the general strike on both tram operations and the economy of the area, and a loss of £500 out of a total of £2,355 does not seem excessive. Undoubtedly a major difficulty was the lasting antipathy of South Shields Corporation towards BET, which it regarded as an arch-capitalist in an area where capitalism had been tried and found wanting. A Shields tradition to be continued on its buses was that of naming tramcars; some were named after Roman emperors, others after ships launched on the Tyne, while early buses carried the more down-to-earth names of steam tugs, such as *Industry* and *High flyer*. One tram, unfortunately named *Mauretania*, upset the local residents who had built its namesake by having a warning siren whose sound was particularly offensive.

At Sunderland there was no increase in the system after 1904 until the Durham Road line of 1925. When a new general manager, Charles A. Hopkins, was appointed in 1929 it was expected that he would recommend abandonment of the deteriorating tramway, having just carried out such an exercise in Wigan. To everyone's surprise he proposed its continuation, indeed extension, and Sunderland was to remain loyal to the tram later than any other north-eastern town. It was on Sunderland trams, too, that the famous exhortation to 'Shop at Binns' originated. This very old-established local store had dabbled in transport advertising with a sign at Tyne Dock station in 1908, and from 1921 had trams fitted with an enamelled iron sign at each end. Before long Northern and United buses carried similar signs, but because of their lower weight used transfers rather than iron plates; in the 1920s Binns purchased existing stores in Middlesbrough, Hartlepool, South Shields and Newcastle, and made sure that the public in each of those towns was similarly advised. Since 1953 Binns has been part of the House of Fraser group, but stores trading under the name Binns have been established in such places as Hull and Harrogate, leading to recent appearances of the slogan there also.

The First Buses

Newcastle was again the earliest and most vigorous in developing the motor bus. The first, introduced in May 1912, ran from Fenham Barracks to Westerhope and was probably a petrol-electric vehicle. The war effort put an end to more routes on the north-east side of the city to Benton, Killingworth and Annitsford which ran for a short time in 1915–16; however, the Westerhope service continued, using gas-powered vehicles. When in the first months of 1919, the Benton routes were re-introduced and extended, a Sentinel steam bus and trailer were used which, it is said, removed manure over the weekend from the Corporation stables, then being cleaned ready for use on Monday morning.

All the routes thus far were to pit villages and began at the tram termini; the first bus to run from the city centre was to Ponteland, which started in June 1921. Westwards they turned at the Scotswood tram terminus, as the *Newcastle Chronicle* had told its readers in August 1920:

> The management of the Newcastle City Tramways are not losing any time in arranging the additional travelling facilities which the Parliamentary Bill gave them power to provide. The omnibus service from Scotswood Bridge to Blaydon and

Ryton is to be inaugurated on Friday with one double-deck bus on each route. A fifteen-minute service will be provided between the bridge and Blaydon, and an hourly service on the Ryton route.

It has been a matter of considerable difficulty for the management to secure the necessary buses, and they recognise that the services at the outset may not be adequate to the needs of the population. As soon as more vehicles can be obtained, they will be at once put into the service.

Optimism was justified, and the Blue Buses, so called in view of their colour scheme, which contrasted with the maroon-and-orange of the trams, were soon running to Branch End and, by August 1925, to Hexham. While north of the city competition from United was keen, on this route the Corporation faced the 'Blaydon A' association, always referred to tersely as 'the opposition'. A diary records:

New Blue Bus service inaugurated 8.30 p.m. Newcastle to Branch End after return from Hexham following a demonstration run via the route. Opposition buses paraded in full force at Scotswood Bridge and travelled in front of the Corporation buses moving very slowly and blocking all progress. 1½ hours late in arriving at Hexham. Service was started following morning properly and were well patronised. Opposition buses having very poor loads.

For two months Blue Buses had been running beyond Ponteland as far as Belsay, and now NCT bought the business of R. Emmerson, who ran from the Westgate terminus to Hexham along the north bank of the Tyne. All these destinations were, of course, well beyond the city boundary and therefore required ministry approval, which the Corporation had neglected to obtain. It now belatedly applied for authority, and the inquiry which followed the objections of Northern, the Blaydon A and the LNER withheld sanction for the Hexham, Belsay and Dudley runs. Newcastle could, however, run as far as Heddon-on-the-Wall on the Hexham route, and did so, while Emmerson resumed the through service and later in 1927 extended it to Carlisle. In February 1929 an agreement was made with the LNER, which by that time had bought out Emmerson, that the latter should run to Heddon and NCT be confined within the city; in return the LNER agreed not to compete along the West Road or on the Throckley tramway.

South of the river a fares war began in July 1927. NCT introduced return tickets, whereupon Blaydon A reduced its fares by a penny immediately, and by a further penny a month later. In May 1929 Corporation fares were reduced, whereupon the opposition issued cheaper weekly passes, but the end was near; in the following March they were bought out for £15,000. Competition, not least from United on the Northumberland routes, made it desirable to bring all the bus routes into the city centre, and this policy was followed from 1925. The Fawdon Bus Co, which began running into the city from the suburbs in 1927, was forced to reduce its frequency by a competing NCT bus service a year later, and sold out in July 1930. The following years saw considerable expansion of buses into new estates.

The two smaller towns were not so ambitious. South Shields' first bus, known as the 'Red Sardine' or 'Harton Boneshaker', plied between the tram route at Stanhope Road and the outer suburbs at Simonside just before war broke out in 1914. In fact the four vehicles involved were not petrol-engined, but carried Edison accumulators enabling them to travel 45 miles between charges; this was very useful during the petrol shortage of the war years, but the batteries could not be replaced either and the buses were converted into conventional vehicles after 1918.

A second route, to Boldon Colliery, commenced in 1921 but was never successful. Northern provided competition, as it did, together with the NER, to Simonside; in 1925 losses at 7d (3p) per mile were equal to revenue, and residents were complaining that the buses threw up stones which broke their windows. Even so, new services to Harton and Cleadon were introduced up to 1929 and the boneshakers were replaced by pneumatic-tyred buses. Increasingly worried about its competitors, SSCT asked the public to 'Travel by chocolate and cream Corporation buses, distinguished at night by a GREEN HEADLIGHT.' The watch committee, which issued bus licences, was evidently not impressed, since it was happy to sanction independents. When it agreed to the 'Royal Red' changing hands, which competed on the Boldon route, the tramway committee chairman retorted: 'If you want us always to be bankrupt, all you have to do is to go on licensing buses.' By 1929 147 buses were licensed, only 11 of them belonging to the Corporation. A ministry inquiry settled matters by fixing routes, stops and fares for the outsiders; their charges were fixed at a level to protect the trams, though not Corporation buses, and Northern was given a clear run to Boldon Colliery, the only route to venture outside the Borough.

Sunderland was later still in the bus field. The Corporation Act of 1927, besides extending the boundary, gave bus operating powers, but when the first routes began the following year buses and crews were hired from Northern for the purpose. In 1929 the first Leyland Lion single-deckers were purchased; two years later there were 21 single and four double-deckers. They were used on the poor Docks tram route, across the suburbs from Fulwell to Humbledon (these were the two that Northern had been running), and to Castletown, a joint route. Hopkins' decision to retain trams did not exclude the use of buses where trams could not be justified, leading to a rapid increase as housing and the borough boundary pushed outwards.

The failure of the two Corporations to link South Shields and Sunderland enabled Northern to run an inland route through Cleadon, but left residents of the coastal mining village of Whitburn without road transport. To fill this gap various individuals ran to the Sunderland tram terminus at Seaburn, using horse-traps, until about 1918, and from then on old ambulances which could carry between six and a dozen passengers. A taxi-rank system was worked, with each vehicle leaving when it was full. One such was owned by G. R. Anderson and E. W. Wilson, who named it *Economic*; it had the advantage of a larger capacity than the others, but it followed that waiting for full loads was impractical. The two partners persisted in the alternative of running to a timetable, invested their profits in more buses (which broke down relations with their competitors, especially at a time when customers were short), and achieved a monopoly by 1927. A year earlier they had started continuing north-wards along the clifftop toll road from Whitburn to Marsden, then turning inland to the centre of South Shields.

One local measure to relieve unemployment at the time was the replacement of the toll road by a new one, which extended almost to the Pier. This enabled Economic buses to run in a loop in South Shields, alternate journeys entering along the Coast Road and returning via Horsley Hill or vice versa. The partners

BEGINNING: R. Tait's Chevrolet (note the curtains and roof-rack) bought in 1928 for his Newcastle-Knowesgate route. The small boy is Tait junior, successor to the business.   *R. Tait*

AND END: The conductor of Rochester & Marshall's last bus from Woodburn to Newcastle, largely the same route as the above, hands leaflets to passengers as, suitably decorated, the bus stands behind.   *Newcastle Journal*

Getting on the bus in South
Shields. The Corporation, faced
with many competitors, went out of
its way in the 1920s to attract
custom.   *Tyne & Wear PTE*

Getting on the bus in Durham.
The original bus station of the
1920s soon outgrew itself and when
seen here in the late 1950s was
congested as usual; single-deck
Bristols of United block the passage
of an SDO Leyland.
          Northern General Transport Co

still had to secure an entrée to Sunderland where the Corporation was opposed to independents; Anderson and Wilson took advantage of the period in 1929 before Hopkins took up his post to obtain a licence. Once their through service started, tram takings were affected so badly that the Council was persuaded to revoke the licence on grounds that Economic paid substandard wages, but the partners meanwhile commenced paying trade union rates, and won a ministry appeal against the revocation. Soon after, Anderson and Wilson took the uncharacteristic step of separating their interests; henceforward 'Economic' was to be simply a name used in common by two distinct businesses in the same way as 'Diamond' further south, and, similarly, schedules were alternated. There was also a close similarity with Gillett and Baker, both in the brown and cream colour scheme used, and in the owner's name at the rear being the only distinguishing feature.

Trolleybuses: Newcastle and South Shields

By the early 1930s Newcastle faced the familiar problem of tramway equipment needing replacement. Buses were proposed for one route in Jesmond, but residents of the then affluent Osborne Road evidently found trams more socially acceptable, and the tracks were expensively patched up. Municipally-generated electricity had its usual appeal, there being a power station next to the offices in Manors, and the decision was made to replace most of the trams by trolleybuses. On the outskirts the opportunity was often taken to run into new housing estates which had initially been served by motor buses.

The first conversion, of the Denton Burn-Wallsend route in October 1935, resulted in a 26 per cent increase in passengers and assured the continuation of the programme; although the Spital Tongues and Westmorland Road lines were converted direct to buses, the transport committee recommended in 1939 that all remaining trams should be replaced by trolleys except in Gosforth Park. However, it was impossible to go ahead with the next stage until 1944, when utility and second-hand trolleys became available. After wartime delay the need to abandon the trams was more urgent than before, as evidenced by Newburn UDC's protests to the City about the Throckley line. This and

119

two others were handed over directly to buses, but as new trolleys arrived in 1949/50 they were used for the remaining tram routes to the east, balancing the earlier conversions which had mostly been in the west. The last tram route wholly in the city, to Scotswood Bridge, received motor buses in 1949, leaving the Gateshead joint services. It had been anticipated that Gateshead would change to trolleys also, and provision for using them across the bridges had been made in the 1945 and 1946 Acts authorising conversion, but this was not to be, and the last Newcastle trams, running over the Tyne bridge, were replaced by motor buses in March 1950. Even then Gateshead trams still ran into Newcastle over the High Level bridge until their abandonment a year later.

The trolleybus routes did not reach a maximum of 37 miles until 1958, although the last extension for normal purposes was in 1950. Six years later the new Slatyford depot in the west of the city was opened, replacing a garage in Wingrove Road, which dated from 1903, and advantage was taken of the necessary wiring to give a regular service. Finally it appeared in the east end at Fossway, but this was because services along the parallel Shields Road were liable to interruption by a railway crossing the road from one part of Parsons engineering works to another, and Parsons paid the bill. Adjoining Parsons was NCT's works and main garage at Byker, where many of the trams had been built; after the Haymarket city centre depot was sold in 1957, Byker was to accommodate two-thirds of the fleet and Slatyford one-third.

The last 70 trolleys, received in 1948/49, were unusual in being of the design always associated with London, the first 20 having in fact been ordered by London Transport but diverted to Newcastle. At this time also the varying liveries disappeared; the tram maroon and orange was no longer to be seen, while motor buses, still blue, but darker than in the 1930s, changed to the trolley scheme of cadmium yellow and cream.

At South Shields trolleys were chosen for the rather different reason that the general manager of the day, E. R. L. Fitzpayne, decided they could best cope with the very rapid housing development. The first route, in October 1936, in fact replaced motor buses rather than trams; it was 1937 before the first tram route, that to Stanhope Road, was converted, and the original Tyne Dock figure-of-eight followed the next year. Now only the

Cleadon line remained, but a greater priority was to introduce trolleys on completely new routes; these were along the Coast Road to Marsden, and to Horsley Hill, introduced in 1938 and 1942 respectively, where of course Economic was a sitting tenant. In 1939 the mileage operated by Corporation vehicles was:

Trolleys	1,238,248
Buses	519,085
Trams	310,311

The trolley proportion was higher still after 1946, when it included the Cleadon mileage, and in 1949 58 trolleys were owned against 33 buses.

Thus the electric vehicle was well entrenched at South Shields. In 1956/7 the Corporation was sufficiently committed to it to buy 12 second-hand trolleys from Pontypridd and St Helens, but at the same time J. Crawford, the general manager from 1949, urged conversion of the Marsden route to buses. This seems to have been a matter of municipal pride, since in the face of Economic competition and with the North Sea to one side of the road, it carried generally poor loads and ran only half-hourly. Technical problems also existed with the overhead equipment, and salt spray caused corrosion in the carbon inserts on the trolleys, so that in winter they had to be replaced four times a day against a normal life of seven days. This special case was accepted by the committee, but when in 1959 a general recommendation to go over to diesels was made, the decision was deferred for two years; a strong preference for coal-generated electricity remained, and it was felt that in future nuclear power might make it available more cheaply. By 1961 Crawford could point to road works as a reason for converting the Cleadon route, and calculated for good measure that the total electricity consumption of Shields trolleys gave employment to $10\frac{1}{2}$ miners. In February 1962 abandonment of the remainder was agreed, and when, two years later, R. E. Bottrill arrived after Crawford's retirement, he urged successfully that the programme be completed within six months, involving basically the figure-of-eight, to fit in with further road works.

Similar considerations decided the fate of Newcastle's trolleys. The city's redevelopment plan, published in 1963, envisaged the closure and realignment of streets; to re-route the trolleybuses would be prohibitively expensive, and diesels could also more easily be accommodated in new housing estates. The first to go in June 1963 was the original route of 1935 between Denton Square and Wallsend, but this time the programme was to be of much shorter duration. A fleet of 200 was replaced by October 1966, with large areas being dealt with simultaneously, notably in May 1965 when nine routes were converted. This considerable achievement was to the credit of Frank S. Taylor, general manager from 1949, who enhanced a tradition of strong finances. The system had never shown a loss, and surpluses in its first 50 years totalled £½ million; between 1956 and 1966 a further £1½ million was ploughed back. Taylor had considerable faith in the Leyland Atlantean, which Newcastle had been buying since 1959 and which was used to replace all the trolleys; by 1971 it was the first major fleet in the country to run only buses of the rear-engined type.

Sunderland and One-Man Operation

At Sunderland Charles Hopkins died in 1948, but the Corporation had already approved his recommendation that the trams be replaced. During the 1930s the system was extended, and in 1938 Hopkins rejected the idea of trolleybuses, which were then appearing in Newcastle and South Shields, but he had the foresight to appreciate that increased post-war traffic and trams would not mix, and that the removal of the town centre population to the outskirts would leave the intensive tram routes under-patronised. At the same time all the available buses were required for the new estates, and the Durham Road line was extended to the boundary in 1949, but this was to be the end. Hopkins' successor, H. W. Snowball, previously his assistant, died in 1952 and was followed by Norman Morton, who, immediately before coming to Sunderland and most unusually for a busman, had worked in road haulage. Meanwhile two short tram routes were converted, but Morton on his arrival decided on a more rapid programme; the last trams ran on the Seaburn line on 1 October 1954.

At this time the Corporation's premises underwent change too. A depot at the Wheatsheaf, Monkwearmouth had been inherited from the horse tram operator, to which was added in

1903 another at Hylton Road. When buses first appeared in 1928 an empty factory in Fulwell was used, where all buses were kept until, after the trams went, Hylton Road was adapted for them. Once these two were in use the Wheatsheaf became solely offices and workshops.

The Corporation had always run some single-deckers, and Morton introduced the first one-man buses in November 1953 on the Hill View route, which was loss-making but important in serving a hospital. The experiment included charging a standard or flat fare of 2d and as it was considered successful, centre-exit Guys were purchased the following year; a further inter-surburban omo route began in 1955, but trade union resistance prevented any further development until the early 1960s, when some lightly loaded double-deck services and one new route were accepted. At this stage there were 183 buses, of which 25 were one-man operated.

In 1963, with increasing fares and declining traffic, a policy of support from rates was agreed, and between 1964 and 1966 the subsidy increased from £20,629 to £80,871. Morton now produced his master plan: the entire fleet was to be converted to large capacity standee single-deckers, a policy made easier since the buses which had replaced the trams were now due to go. To enable them to be one-man operated the same fare of 4d would be charged for any journey, or passengers could buy tokens in bulk at a discount in advance. He argued that this would both encourage traffic from the outer suburbs, where there was a higher ratio of cars to buses, and protect the families who had been rehoused compulsorily by the Council in those suburbs.

With Council support, the system was introduced in September 1966, but the immediate effect in 1967 was a loss of £196,000. There was another difficulty which was not to be resolved; when in 1952 the Borough boundary had been extended to include some Northern territory, agreement had been reached that the estates involved would be served on a 50/50 basis by Corporation and company. Northern was naturally reluctant to charge fares which were well below its normal scale, and the tokens could not be used on its buses, a powerful deterrent to passengers on routes where either a red or a green bus might turn up.

The Corporation had probably realised that as the licensing system worked, it had a useful means of keeping Northern fares down; by subsidising its own buses from the rates, it obliged Company buses to charge the same low fares on common routes. Northern's chairman, A. F. R. Carling, complained at the 1967 annual general meeting that if the Sunderland subsidy was extended to all Northern buses it would cost £1,200,000 a year. At this stage fate took a hand. In the 1967 municipal elections, the Labour group which had controlled Sunderland since 1946 was defeated by Conservatives opposed to subsidy. An application was made to increase the flat fare, when the Corporation was urged by both Northern and the traffic commissioners to revert to more conventional charging. The change was made in January 1969 to a zonal system, where passengers paid a standard fare or token for each section of the route; this was against Morton's advice and he resigned, and died not long afterwards.

To replace him R. E. Bottrill moved from South Shields. He favoured the retention of the token/zonal system and the one-man programme continued, but finances improved little. Most important, there was a serious decline in traffic, from 80 million passengers in 1962 to 46 million in 1972, which may have been due to unreliability of the new buses, possibly to their utilitarian nature and the likelihood of having to stand, or perhaps to the reduction in frequency resulting from driver shortages. This was good material for F. S. Taylor in Newcastle, when the city planning officer put forward ideas for reducing traffic congestion by the use of more one-man operation, tokens, more frequent services, and subsidies to keep fares artificially low. Besides disagreeing with the theory that low fares would attract passengers, and suggesting that more frequent one-man buses did not ease congestion, he pointed to the Sunderland experience of greater losses from them.

Not that Newcastle and South Shields ignored omo. Both had been running entirely double-deck fleets for some years, but re-introduced single-deck vehicles in 1967. Neither had any particularly quiet routes, and it was clear that if more one-man buses were to be run, they must be double-deckers; Newcastle therefore rebuilt an Atlantean at Byker to incorporate a centre exit in 1968, and this became the standard design for future buses. There was nothing new about it, since the first trolleybuses, with entrances at the rear, had incorporated front exits to speed the flow of passengers.

Passenger Transport Executive

The Transport Act, 1968 decreed that in the four major conurbations outside London new bodies should take over the fleets of the various municipal operators, mainly in the interests of simplification and to enable public transport to be part of overall planning. Neither of these objectives would easily be achieved in the case of Tyneside, where the two municipal operators' routes did not meet and a high proportion of the buses were owned by companies and independents.

While the Labour group on Newcastle City Council favoured the proposal, and advocated its extension to the whole territory of the 1948 area scheme, the controlling Conservative group disagreed. Alderman Neville Trotter, chairman of the traffic, highways and transport committee, wrote:

> The existence of so many local authorities on Tyneside hinders planning for the conurbation as a whole, and the City Council appreciate that the new concept of a Passenger Transport Authority with its professional Executive can serve a useful role in the wider sphere of transport policy.
>
> The Council has, however, doubted the wisdom or necessity of the Executive taking over the operation of the City bus fleet, especially as the buses of the other operators on Tyneside will not be taken over ...
>
> In the meantime, we must hope that the new Executive will produce advantages to outweigh the disadvantages and the City Council, in the interests of the travelling public, wish the Executive every success.

Trotter was soon to have more ammunition; the Passenger Transport Authority, consisting of elected representatives from the various local authorities, had as one of its first tasks to choose a chairman, and then a director-general for the PTE. While Newcastle was Conservative, the bulk of the other authorities were Labour, with the effect that the decisions were made by interests unconnected with the fleet which made up three-quarters of its assets. The chairman elected, in April 1969, was Alderman Andrew Cunningham, a member of the Labour Party National Executive and a Durham County Councillor, where again there were no PTE operations, and it was arranged that the sub-committee which chose the director-general contained no Newcastle representatives at all. After six weeks, in which time further wrangling took place between party factions in Newcastle over the choice of a general manager to succeed Taylor until the PTE took over, Dr. T. M. Ridley was elected director-general. As a Wearsider who had obtained a doctorate in civil engineering in California, his appointment followed criticism in the technical press of non-busmen being chosen. Cunningham said, 'I think we have made the best choice from a short-list of extremely capable candidates', but Trotter was not so sure:

> He is a very brainy backroom boy, well versed in the theory of transport. It will be interesting to see how he deals with the management of a very large transport undertaking as he has had no management experience whatever, or experience of financial control.

In the event Trotter had no need to worry. The press had failed to appreciate that the PTE were more than large bus organisations, having a responsibility for overall transport planning in the conurbations, and Tyneside's record was to be as good as any. Dr Ridley's background encouraged the reorganisation of the bus network which, like many municipalities, still 'followed the tramlines' and tended to ignore changes in travel patterns. An old NCT practice of running express services to Gosforth was revived in the form of limited stop routes to Killingworth and Kingston Park, using coaches whose utilisation was increased by the promotion of private hire work. In the long term the whole system will be geared to a Metro rapid transit railway network consisting of existing suburban lines and a new underground section in central Newcastle and Gateshead, linked by a new bridge over the Tyne.

However, not everything was rosy. The labour unrest in the industry at the time spread to Tyneside too, and was probably aggravated by uncertainty as to the PTE's intentions. Staff were particularly unhappy in South Shields, where there was a long history of local political interest in the transport undertaking. As early as 1933 an accusation that an employee had been sacked to accommodate an Alderman's relation led to the resignation of a competent manager, J. Austin Baker; there was continuing suspicion of councillors taking free rides, and in 1952 there was a strike because a clerical post went to a municipal rent collector rather than an experienced transport man. Contrary to Newcastle, the town welcomed the 1948 area schemes in the hope that some autonomy would be retained together with control over Northern's activities. In a final characteristic gesture, when most other municipalities struck in 1967 against the Government's wages policy and the freezing of the 'busman's pound', South Shields men opposed the policy of their own union 'out of loyalty to the Labour Government'. Now the valued local undertaking was seen to be a poor relation of distant Newcastle, whose 350 buses swamped the 86 in Shields, and, unfortunately in the circumstances, it was decided that Newcastle yellow should be adopted as the PTE colour scheme, so replacing the traditional blue.

Under the 1972 Local Government Act a new County of Tyne & Wear was created, whose Council replaced the PTA; the effect, of course, was to add Sunderland Corporation to the yellow PTE fleet from April 1974, and in place of two entirely separate operations there were now three. The situation where, previously, services between Newcastle and South Shields were provided by Northern, now applied between all three, but quite uniquely the most frequent route between Shields and Sunderland was still that of the independent Economic. It was not a great surprise when the PTE acquired the two businesses concerned in January 1975. Sunderland also has the unusual feature of an independent running entirely within the town; this was A. L. and K. K. Jolly, who originally had run from South Hylton to the tram terminus at Kayll Road. Jolly had gradually lost traffic to the Corporation as the boundary was extended, housing estates were built around the previous village of South Hylton, and direct Corporation buses extended to serve them. In 1964, however, justice was done when the Durham-Sunderland railway closed, involving a station at Hylton, and Jolly successfully applied to run his frequent service through to the town centre as a replacement.

Tyne & Wear PTE, as it was retitled, had next to get to grips with the Sunderland problem. The Corporation had not increased its fares since 1970, resulting in a deficit in 1973 of no less than £698,000, which had been made up from the rates; it was clear also that low fares had not been an attraction, since revenue was declining by £100,000 a year. As soon as possible

127

fares were increased by half, and later in 1974 the zonal fare system and tokens were replaced by conventional methods. The bold Sunderland experiment had failed, and came to an end.

On Tyneside the PTE, after its teething troubles, moved confidently ahead. Maps and timetables made available to the public, in some cases for the first time, were part of a policy to increase public awareness and information. The yellow buses, still hand-painted and varnished and kept clean in all but the worst Tyneside weather, impress by their sheer numbers in the city centre and brighten the red-brick terraces of Elswick, Wallsend and Westoe. The new Metro rail system with its yellow painted articulated electric trains will herald a new era in Tyneside transport and will be watched with interest from other parts of the country. It will be unique in Britain although becoming more common on the European mainland, for the Metro combines the best features of modern rail technology, drawing on a long history of conventional heavyweight railways and lightweight tramways, which 20 years ago were thought to have disappeared for ever.

6

THE TEESSIDE MUNICIPALITIES

Trams and Trolleybuses

Comparable industrial development to that of Tyneside and Wearside was going on in the 1870s around the mouth of the Tees. Although the estuary was similar in its use for the transport of coal from South Durham, the Cleveland ore led additionally to the establishment of major iron works away from the established communities; in turn new industrial towns emerged, at West Hartlepool and Middlesbrough, which were to eclipse the established centres at Hartlepool and Stockton.

Public transport was first offered locally in Middlesbrough by horse trams, which changed hands and were converted to steam traction before coming into the hands of the Imperial Tramways Company in 1896. Imperial was a holding company based in Bristol; trams in Bristol were provided by one of its subsidiaries and the company had ambitions akin to those of BET. It electrified and linked up the Teesside operations to form two routes; one began in Norton, a northern suburb of Stockton, and ran through the town, crossing the Tees and passing through Thornaby and Middlesbrough before terminating at North Ormesby on the south bank, while the other was a local line from Linthorpe to the transporter bridge, which crossed the first in the centre of Middlesbrough. (The transporter, a masterpiece of Victorian engineering, remains to this day the most direct link between Middlesbrough and the north bank. It is therefore an important part of Teesside's transport network, though outdated and locally a source of frustration and amusement. Responsibility for its operation has passed from Middlesbrough Corporation to its public transport successors.)

Imperial's tramway mileage remained static, development being instead in the form of buses. It is uncertain where these ran, though probably they were to the south of Stockton. At any rate they were not east of Middlesbrough, where stretching almost continuously through Grangetown to Redcar was a mighty concentration of heavy industry which drew much of its labour from Middlesbrough but, apart from the Middlesbrough-Saltburn railway, had no public transport at all. As a result Messrs Bolckow Vaughan, later part of the Dorman Long steel company, took the philanthropic step of promoting the North Ormesby Act of 1912 to provide a service from the tram terminus to Eston and Grangetown, and most unusually at this early date the vehicles were to be 'trackless', ie trolleybuses.

However, their performance was less than their intention. The south bank was still relatively uncharted territory as far as road transport was concerned, with many complications in the form of tollgates and rights-of-way, and once these were dealt with the first world war prevented further action. As soon as hostilities were over the two local authorities concerned, Middlesbrough Corporation and Eston UDC, obtained powers to run the system through a joint board, in which they had respectively one-third and two-thirds shares. It duly completed and the Teesside Railless Traction Board began operations in November 1919.

A Hartlepools Steam Tramways Co Ltd started business in 1884 with a line linking the old part of Hartlepool (the headland) with the growing West, but there was not yet sufficient population to support both it and the existing branch of the North Eastern Railway, and it closed in 1891. Four years later the line was purchased by the General Electric Tramways Company, an offshoot of the embryo BET, which leased it to the Hartlepool Electric Tramways Company, another subsidiary; it was one of BET's first four purchases and the first electric tramway in the North East. More tracks were laid to the seaside suburb of Seaton Carew, to the Park and to Foggy Furze, an aptly-named area adjoining the South Durham Steel Works, before West Hartlepool Corporation took over ownership of its portion of the track and all the assets in 1911/12. The HET was then wound up, but GET continued to be the owner of the $1\frac{1}{4}$ miles of track in the territory of the separate Hartlepool Corporation.

The scene was set for the first confrontation between the rival local authorities. West Hartlepool was faced with heavy expenditure on the tramway if it was to be retained after 1918, and decided instead to use trolleybuses, converting the internal routes between 1924 and 1927. Across the boundary it intended a longer trolley route, which Hartlepool countered with proposals for local and overlapping motor buses. The wishes of GET, which, as owner of the track, was due to negotiate its lease, were ignored. Following discussions in Parliament in June 1925, it was resolved that Hartlepool should buy out GETs interest in the track and obtain trolleybus powers. In February 1927 they duly appeared, still operated entirely by West Hartlepool, as in tram days, but with the West Hartlepool now paying its lessee's rent to Hartlepool in respect of the mileage within it.

The 1920s and 1930s: The Bus Takes Over

The trend towards direct ownership of trams was the principal reason why Imperial did not survive as long as BET. In 1921 the three municipalities involved, Stockton, Thornaby and Middlesbrough, jointly purchased the local system. Imperial lost its other interests, and after it had gone into liquidation in 1930, Bristol Tramways passed to the Tilling group by way of Great Western Railway interests and Western National.

Stockton and Thornaby were in favour of the three authorities operating a joint undertaking, but as Middlesbrough did not share their views separate organisations were set up; Thornaby, however, did not wish to run its own trams and formed a joint committee with Stockton, which was responsible for management. The two authorities rapidly built up bus fleets alongside the trams and found, as might be expected, that considerable joint operation was necessary because of traffic between the towns. By 1930 Stockton had a fleet of 43 buses, with the demand for workers' traffic so great that 30 of these were needed only for peak operation. Much of the growth was at the works of the Synthetic Ammonia Company, north of Stockton in the new town of Billingham, later to become Imperial Chemical Industries; this, of course, attracted its labour from the south bank of the Tees as well as the north, and it became necessary for Middlesbrough to be involved. At the time of the Road Traffic Act Stockton buses were running south of the town to Yarm and High Leven, and north into Billingham, while Middlesbrough ventured as far as Stokesley.

Amid this expansion the remaining tramway, although profitable, compared unfavourably and attracted a steady flow of criticism in the local press. The partners decided on abandonment in 1931, and converted the main line the next year and the Linthorpe-Transporter branch in 1934; Thornaby, having lost with ownership of the track its last tangible interest, sold its share to Stockton.

The Teesside board was also finding the bus more attractive. In response to passengers who complained of the change at North Ormesby a motor bus service was introduced in 1929 from Eston to Middlesbrough, although as early as 1924 the board had experimented with a petrol electric vehicle which ran on the wires from South Bank to Normanby and then as a motor bus to Eston. The general manager of the day, J. B. Parker, in fact urged the board to abandon trolleybuses entirely, at a time when most towns had not yet introduced them, but his advice was not taken, surprising again, perhaps, when Middlesbrough seems never seriously to have considered the trolley.

West Hartlepool decided to use buses to link its tram terminus at Seaton Carew with the Transporter, bringing passengers within walking distance of the centre of Middlesbrough. It started running jointly with Middlesbrough in 1921 after, it appears, using these buses temporarily on a local route within West Hartlepool, while Stockton began its own route along the north bank. Because of the shortage of traffic offering, the route consisting mostly of mud-flats, small AEC's were used and successful experiments made with one-man operation; the summer holiday traffic to Seaton Carew was such that some of the first buses were used in winter to try new suburban routes, which led to more one-man buses within the town and for special duties such as school, theatre and cinema traffic.

By 1930, now running through from West Hartlepool to Port Clarence, after Middlesbrough dropped out in 1927, 16 buses were operated, but the Road Traffic Act effectively prevented the use of buses carrying more than 20 people without a conductor. In any case, since the staff opposed the idea of one-man trolleybuses on grounds that conductors would be made redundant, there were clearly limitations. In the light of events 30 years later it is interesting that, most unusually for a municipality, all the single-deck buses bought between 1925 and 1935 were Bristols. From 1931 double-deckers were mostly used in preference, but they were to be Daimlers until the war; in 1934 it was decided to change the previous livery of chocolate and white to dominion red and cream, said closely to resemble the colours of a local shipowner who was chairman of the transport committee.

The man of the decade was Frank Lythgoe, Middlesbrough's general manager from 1935. His undertaking was in deficit after the tram abandonment, which he set about turning ruthlessly

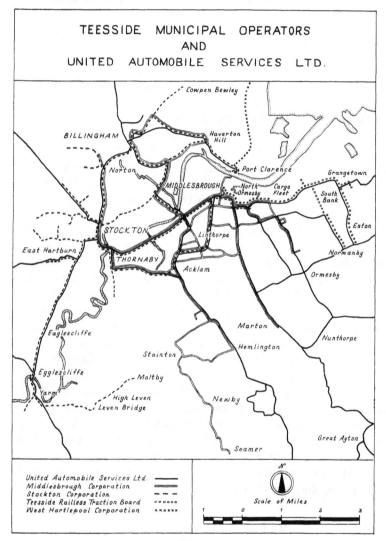

Fig. 4

into surplus. First he observed that there were 'many dead limbs to be pruned', the payroll economies that resulted in savings of £180 per week; the staff that remained were instructed in the better performance of their jobs, and encouraged by notices exhibited around the premises:

Conscientious work is essential for Enjoyable Leisure — The Law of Life.
Be considerate. You may need help yourself one day. Honest Work is the Best Policy.

He reduced frequencies, changed maintenance practices, and speeded up services to bring the fleet down from 60 to 40 buses. Believing that it was bad practice to allow standing time at terminals, he abolished it with the effect, he claimed, of reducing accidents and staff sickness, apparently because there was no time for a smoke between journeys. These changes naturally attracted opposition, but the times were not favourable; when Hopkins' similar proposals at Sunderland met with objections from employees, he had only to threaten dismissal of anyone who struck to remove them.

Commendably, Lythgoe arranged for publicity regarding his timetable changes to be distributed to every house in the town, and invited suggestions from the public, but rather ingenuously he was disappointed in human nature when all the suggestions would improve facilities only for the very people who wrote. He did not, however, look far outside the town. While both Middlesbrough and Stockton made the familiar protection agreements with United, in some cases favouring the company, and in 1938 H. Franklin's Panther Services from Stainton and Seamer were taken over, there were no clear operating territories. United was not prevented from developing on the outskirts and, equally important, the municipalities were slow to appreciate the growth of travel between the towns; in this way an unusual pattern emerged where, even along the established joint municipal routes, the company was allowed to develop frequent services on the fringes of Middlesbrough and Billingham, and between them.

Reorganisation and Change

As prosperity began to return, West Hartlepool invested in

MADE TO MEASURE: An East Yorkshire Leyland Titan, with 'Gothic' roof to allow passage through the North Bar at Beverley, shows how tight a fit it remained. *Hull Daily Mail*

Six AEC Renowns, received by Tynemouth in 1972 in exchange for Daimlers sent to East Yorkshire, had a slight 'Beverley Bar' taper. For a short time they carried the attractive maroon and cream colour scheme shown.

Northern General Transport Co

CHANGES IN DOUBLE-DECK DESIGN. This Tynemouth Guy Arab was used by the Northern General group in 1950 to reinforce its anti-nationalisation campaign of the time. *Northern General Transport Co*

Nearly 30 more passengers could be carried in a Leyland Atlantean such as this specimen owned by OK Motor Services. It waits to leave Bishop Auckland for Newcastle when new in 1973. *C.S. Marshall*

modernisation of the fleet. Charles Hopkins, who acted as consultant, recommended increased use of the trolleybus, but in fact the opposite was to happen. The Foggy Furze route was to be extended to Seaton Carew, under a low railway bridge which could be negotiated by double-deck buses but not by trolleybuses; it was intended to use diesels until more single-deck trolleys could be obtained, which they never were. So in 1938 the first trolleybus conversion was made, probably fortunately, since wartime circumstances were to require services from various parts of the town to factories and shipyards, work which trolleys could not do.

Once the war was over the Corporation decided to change to buses over the whole system, where already they outnumbered trolleys by two to one. The first choice, in 1949, was the coastal Seaton Carew route, which like Marsden presented technical problems. After this there followed the Park route in 1953, which was associated with the enlargement of the Borough, and the extension of bus routes to the new estates, leaving again only that to Hartlepool, where a drama of the first order was to follow.

The agreement between the two parties expired in April 1953, whereupon West Hartlepool unilaterally placed buses on the route. Hartlepool Corporation thus received no more revenue as owner of the wiring in its territory, but it was determined to retain an interest; motor bus powers had been obtained in 1925 but not used, and it would not have made sense to set up a transport department for the sake of a half share in one route. It turned therefore to United as the remaining major bus operator in the area, which obtained four second-hand Bristols and painted them in the chosen colours of blue and cream. At the last minute the crews stated that if they were to run municipal buses on the Corporation's behalf, they must be paid municipal rates, which were higher than their own; this was something United's management could not agree for fear that if it did there would be similar requests where its buses ran over Corporation routes in Middlesbrough and Newcastle. Hartlepool then turned to Bee-Line Roadways, which took over and ran the four blue buses until new ones arrived; after one of the sagas not often recorded, which periodically occur in the bus industry, municipal pride won again.

Rivalry only came to an end in April 1967, when it was

decreed that the two Boroughs should be merged into one, to be known as Hartlepool, and the old music-hall joke of West Hartlepool legally disappeared. Remarkably the two had been able to agree in advance that the joint route should be converted to omo from the takeover date, and even to order similar buses for the purpose. West Hartlepool had introduced one-man buses in 1964 with Leyland Leopards incorporating an advanced driver's cab design which ensured success. From the merger, and recalling events 40 years before, it standardised on Bristol buses with Eastern Coach Works bodies. These two manufacturers, originating with Tilling bus companies, had become State-owned in 1948 and were then only able to supply the BTC subsidiaries, but under the Transport Act, 1962 their products were again available on the open market. Hartlepool was the first municipal buyer after 1962 and when R. E. Bottrill moved from the town to be manager at South Shields the type appeared there also. Such was the success of the West Hartlepool programme and its buses, and by 1967 one-man vehicles ran 42 per cent of total mileage, and in 1976 the 11 double-deckers which remained operated only about eight per cent; the 76 single-deckers are perhaps better suited to the short routes of Hartlepool, where only that to Port Clarence runs outside the borough, than they are to Sunderland.

The remaining operators were merged into one by another local government change. Previously Stockton and Billingham, on the north bank, had been in County Durham while Thornaby, Middlesbrough and Eston were in the North Riding, and a more logical unit was created in April 1968 in the form of Teesside County Borough. It was appropriate that Teesside Municipal Transport chose a turquoise colour scheme to replace the blue of Middlesbrough and the green of TRTB and Stockton. An interesting point was that while Stockton distinguished its routes by numbers, Middlesbrough used letters; where there were joint services they found common ground by making Norton-North Ormesby O, and Billingham-Middlesbrough 11. Similarly the two, together with United, catered for a major area of housing and industrial development in Thornaby after 1962, when the RAF vacated its airfield there; a route I to Middlesbrough was introduced, technically joint but in fact operated by Stockton, although it was entirely outside the borough and another Stockton 1 existed elsewhere.

After the merger the protection agreements with United,

which tended to cancel each other out, were brought to an end except in Billingham, where a complex territorial arrangement continued. The various fare scales also had to be unified, a sensitive area because Middlesbrough in particular had prided itself on its cheap fares and, indeed, on having the last penny fare in the country. Over the years the disparity had been reduced as Middlesbrough, once very densely populated, was redeveloped and became more akin to Stockton.

Teesside had to pay a price for its economic success in the sufferings of its public transport operators from the blandishments of oil and chemical manufacturers. As Thornaby expanded so did its bus services, but it could only be done by transferring facilities from elsewhere; when one factory opened, 34 conductresses left Stockton Corporation in a week to work there. In this situation, where other industries could offer much better wages and conditions, it was not surprising that in 1967 the protest by municipal busmen against the 'freezing of the busmen's pound' became in Middlesbrough a strike lasting 53 days. Fortunately TMT was later able to make rapid progress with one-man operation, mostly with double-deckers, which both reduced staff requirements and raised wage levels. In 1974 about 65 per cent of a fleet of 283 was worked by one-man operation.

There remained the TRTB fleet operating from a depot at South Bank. While more buses were owned than trolleys, the latter ran more than half of the regular service; an extension in Grangetown was made in 1951 and, although the Bill to establish the County Borough provided for abandonment of the trolleybuses, a completed circular route was opened on 31 March 1968 – clearly a final gesture. However, during the winter of 1969/70 mechanical problems and shortage of spare parts forced the use of buses in partial replacement and this brought the end nearer. Britain's penultimate trolleybus system was handed over to buses on 5 April 1971, but strangely most continued to turn at the historic North Ormesby terminus rather than run into Middlesbrough.

Cleveland County

In April 1974 a new county came into being, named after the Cleveland Hills which formed its rural southern boundary and based on Teesside County Borough, but expanded to absorb parts of Durham and the North Riding. Under the Local Government Act municipalities with bus fleets in the shire counties were to continue to control them at District level, as did Darlington. In Cleveland there were to be four Districts, Hartlepool, Stockton, Middlesbrough and Langbaurgh (based on Redcar), so that in theory the fleet would have to be re-divided between Stockton and Middlesbrough. It was felt locally, not least among the transport committees, that there was a case for Cleveland being a Metropolitan County like Tyne & Wear which would, inter alia, have formed the municipal fleets into a PTE and given greater control over United. When it became clear that this was not acceptable to the government, Stockton at first reacted by proposing to withdraw its fleet, but later agreed with Middlesbrough and Langbaurgh to form a joint committee so as to preserve the status quo. Hartlepool, whose only contact with TMT was at the Port Clarence (Transporter) terminus, remained outside, and the new creation, Cleveland Transit, was therefore in practice Teesside Municipal under new colours of green and cream.

It was to be clear, however, that Cleveland took itself seriously. When W. R. Holland became General Manager in 1972 the organisation's style began to change to resemble rather that of a company. First, in January 1973 a limited stop service under the 'Swiftaway' name began from Stockton to Billingham, followed in July by another from Middlesbrough to Acklam and in November by two more from the Transporter to Eston; TMT took the unusual step of buying second-hand double-deck coaches for these services and later new coaches which were also used to develop private hire work.

Most significant of all was the purchase, in August 1974, of Saltburn Motor Services, in a part of the extreme south of the county otherwise served only by United. By coincidence, its proprietor, J. C. Pickering, had been a partner in Cleveland Motor Services, running in the Lingdale/Guisborough area, before purchasing a business operating between Saltburn and Loftus in 1928. This served iron-mining communities so close to the coast at Saltburn that if a fine day turned to rain, villagers would go home and perhaps return if it cleared again. When Pickering was required to obtain a licence in 1930 his rivals objected to his having the freedom he sought to run relief buses

140

at any time; exasperated, the chairman of the traffic commissioners asked, 'Have you no control over the weather at Saltburn?'

Development before and after the second world war was in the coach field, at first with excursions under the name of 'Parlour Coaches', then for building workers to the vast ICI complex at Wilton, which brought the fleet to 44 vehicles. When Wilton was completed there were contracts for chemical employees, workers at the Dorman Long steelworks and schoolchildren. In 1954 Saltburn took over a long route from Saltburn to Thirsk from John Dunning (Green Line), which was later cut back to Stokesley and operated from a garage at Guisborough obtained from another firm, Jackson's Cleveland Coaches, with Teesside contracts. The bus side was further increased in 1956 when a new Saltburn-Skelton route appeared and that to Loftus extended to Moorsholm over a route where Moor-Dale of Newcastle had once run, but over the following years commitments were reduced again.

With a further development into local services in Guisborough run by Midi-Buses, Cleveland Transit seemed to be emerging as more than an urban local bus operator, with interests over much of an admittedly small county. It was also establishing a reputation for engineering experiment by converting a bus to run on liquified petroleum gas, which, with its valuable low-exhaust properties, was regarded as a possible fuel of the future.

Darlington Corporation Transport

Not part of Teesside in the accepted sense, but close to the river's banks 15 miles upstream from the estuary, lies Darlington. In character it is more like Stockton than Middlesbrough, a market town that has had industry thrust upon it. It had also been a staging post on the Great North Road, and gained from this background a well laid out town centre including a large and pleasant market place; this became the hub of the municipal transport system and makes up for the industrial dereliction and squalor of parts of the outskirts.

Darlington became famous as the cradle of the steam railway, and much of its 19th-century prosperity came from the railway workshops, although associated iron manufacturing concerns such as Cleveland Bridge were important too. It is perhaps appropriate, then, that here in 1862 was built the first street tramway in the North East and one of the first in the country. It ran from the Market Place to the North Road station of the Stockton & Darlington Railway, and that company may have had an interest in the tramway, but financial problems caught up with it after three years.

For some years after 1865 a horse bus served the route, but tram working was resumed in 1880 by the Stockton & Darlington Steam Tramways Company. This in turn went into liquidation, to be succeeded by Imperial Tramways, which also, as we have seen, owned the system at the mouth of the Tees. In 1899 application was made for a light railway order, granted in 1902, which permitted electrification of the system, still horse-drawn, and its enlargement to 4·87 miles of route in four directions. At this stage Darlington Corporation took the view that it should secure the undertaking's profit for itself, and to ensure that things went its way bought out Imperial. On 1 June 1904 the Darlington Corporation Light Railway Department began running electric trams on the Harrowgate Hill route (an extension along the original North Road), and three further routes were introduced over the following months.

The system remained unaltered when abandonment was proposed in the early 1920s, for the familiar reason of neglect during the first world war; also, it seems, Edwardian trams were not in keeping with the modern image that was desired for the town. The general manager of Birmingham Tramways, employed as a consultant, recommended trolleybuses which would use municipally-generated electricity and cost 3d a mile less to run than would buses. In April 1926, 24 trolleybuses replaced the trams, and the manager since 1904, J. R. P. Lunn, ruled over the new Gas, Electricity and Transport Department. In 1927 an experiment took place involving the hire of four motor buses, but public reaction was unfavourable.

The trolleybus era was to see considerable expansion, increasing the route mileage from under five to 12 when abandonment began. The remarkable thing is that this was possible while the United company was pursuing a policy of aggressive growth from a headquarters within the town. Certainly offers to purchase were made by United, which replaced Scarborough's trams by buses in 1931, and some elements within the Council would have favoured a sale — an opinion that was still held in the 1950s. The prevailing view, however, was that better local services could be provided by the Corporation being master in its own house. A fleet of trolleybuses contributed to this view in that after 1930, unlike buses, they were not subject to the traffic commissioners' control; such an undertaking was also inherently less attractive to United, and gave some guarantee that it would not compete directly. The route extensions that took place were mostly off main roads into new housing areas that did not conflict with United, which was, in fact, quite happy if local passengers were kept off its longer-distance routes. The usual protection agreement was made in 1935, but, by making United passengers pay higher fares over common routes, its effect was slight. Co-operation between the two parties continued to be the rule.

The first manager retired in 1937; J. S. King observed later: 'He left the department in a very sound condition. Working expenses were only 78 per cent of gross receipts, and a good net profit was made every year. The town was well served by quiet, cheap and comfortable transport.' A manager was sought for a new transport department at £650 a year, and the lucky man was W. H. Penman, previously manager at Perth and Lancaster.

Darlington, as befitted a railway town, was a microcosm of the Durham low bridge problem, and all the Corporation's rolling stock had been single-deck except for a pair of tramcars. After the second world war, in June 1946, the streets committee announced its intention of lowering the road under three of the most vital bridges, encouraging the transport committee to order its first batch of six double-deck trolleybuses.

The hurry was rather unfortunate, for the future of the electric vehicle was itself in doubt. The war had left the wiring in much the same condition as the tramways had been after 1918, while the central terminus area lay in the Great North Road which, until very recent times, passed through the town; traffic congestion was already causing concern and would, it was felt, be lessened if motor buses were used. So on 23 April 1947 the decision was made to convert to diesels over a period.

A way was now sought to exchange the ordered trolleys for diesels, but the Ministry of Transport intervened to point out that under the 1947 Transport Act the undertaking could be nationalised, and it might be wise to delay the decision. Almost as soon as the trolleys arrived in 1949 ministerial blessing was received; the first buses, seven double-deck and three single-deck

143

Guys, arrived in 1950 to be used on new operations until November 1951 when the first trolleybus route was withdrawn. At this stage the double-deck trolleys, unlikely to be used on the intended routes since the bridge works had not proceeded, were sold, and more Guy buses were bought, which had been ordered by Darlington Triumph before selling out. In such a situation Penman was probably glad to retire in 1950 to give way to W. Mayes.

Replacement of the trolleybuses continued over the next six years, the Suez crisis of 1956 delaying the final conversion. Another reason for the decision in favour of diesels had been their adaptability to new housing developments, and in the ten years from 1952 to 1962 the route mileage doubled from 12 to 24. This still low figure, and the short individual route lengths, emphasises the smallness of the Darlington operation by municipal standards; unlike some areas, such as the Tees estuary, there is no conurbation involving several operators, and services have never run outside the immediate built-up area.

Through the 1950s Darlington favoured Guy vehicles, including some unusual centre-entrance single-deckers to cope with the remaining low bridges. The early 1960s saw a change to Daimler, which later in the decade introduced a rear-engined single-deck type, the Roadliner, powered by an American Cummins engine. Since that company had been induced to open a factory in Darlington as part of the Corporation's policy to counter the closure of the railway workshops, it was thought politic to buy the Roadliner, and 12 of the type became the first one-man-operated buses in 1967. In common with other buyers, Darlington found them very unsatisfactory mechanically, and two were scrapped after six years.

This bad start did not delay the one-man programme, and it was Mayes' achievement to have two-thirds of the fleet converted by his retirement in 1972; Daimler standee single-deckers – not Roadliners – were thought suitable for the short journeys made, and as time progressed the double-deckers, which had been predominant around 1960, once again became a minority. Mayes was succeeded by P. A. Ellis, under whom the established policies continued, but before he went, Darlington hit the national headlines in an unusual split between management and the transport committee. In 1971, shortly after a similar affair at Wolverhampton had been settled, a Sikh who applied

144

for employment was refused on the grounds that his turban would prevent him from wearing the regulation uniform. The committee debated the issue, while television cameras were trained on the Houndgate offices, and finally − sensibly − overruled Mayes.

Local government reorganisation on 1 April 1974 was celebrated by the introduction of a new fleetname logo, but little substantial change seems likely. Darlington survives as the only municipal undertaking in Durham, now a District authority with a much larger area than before. In the remainder of the district outside the old County Borough, United has almost a complete monopoly, but as all routes but one continue to destinations outside the district there is little scope or need for development.

7

THE INDEPENDENTS

A history of bus operation in many parts of the country would not need a separate chapter on private operators, since over the years all but a few have disappeared. The North East is one of the areas where, in the late 1970s, independents continue to run important and frequent routes, although even in one of their main centres of activity their combined total of journeys is no more than those of the National Bus Company.

We may ask why so many have survived. There seem to be three principal theories: first, that running buses is financially more rewarding than in other parts, with the examples of the profitable Northern and United companies; second, simple bloody-mindedness, as one Durham operator himself put it; third, that as there were so many in the first place, the process of elimination would take longer. Certainly in the 1920s prodigious numbers of businesses were in existence, and it is doubtful if anyone will ever know of all that ever ran into Bishop Auckland.

The story of the bus business is one of gradual concentration in fewer hands, and in this the North East is not exceptional. We shall see, and have already seen in previous chapters, that the ranks have declined. On the other hand there has been a strong tendency for independents leaving the business to sell to those continuing, especially within the associations, rather than to the large companies, and this has strengthened the position of the survivors. This chapter will be a study of that process in the four main areas of independent activity.

North-West Durham

The hilly and populous mining district around Stanley was good business for many bus proprietors in the early 1920s. Typically they might have begun after 1918 with a single Ford model T, or they might have graduated to motor vehicles from using a pony and trap to collect passengers and goods from the railway station before the war. Usually they went wherever they thought the pickings were best, running housewives into

OPERATORS IN THE 'DIAMOND' ASSOCIATION, 1926-1974

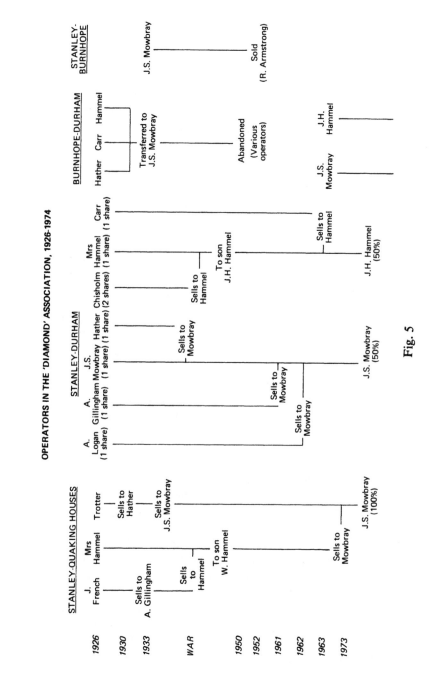

Fig. 5

Durham for shopping and at night perhaps taking cinema crowds home.

By 1926 many of the operators had settled on more or less regular routes and timetables, but realised that there were too many competing for the same traffic; they knew too that passengers would be attracted by a more regular and reliable service. They therefore formed associations by which those in a particular area agreed to run a given timetable while retaining their individual businesses.

The largest was the Diamond group, which originally comprised independents running from Stanley through South Moor to Craghead and Durham or Quaking Houses; on the Durham route there were more operators than the required number of buses, so that each had to find some other use for his bus for part of the time. On the north side of Stanley a similar group was formed known as the Union Bus Service, a name also used by an association running into Durham from the Brandon area. The latter was swallowed up by United in the early 1930s while the Stanley Union came into the hands of S. S. Holmes and Hunter Bros of Tantobie. It so continued until 1959, when Holmes sold his share to the Hunters, who still run the two routes, albeit as second fiddle to a growing haulage business. Finally, G. H. Atkinson of Chester-le-Street joined with D. Finlay of Beamish to form the 'General A' with routes to Grange Villa and to Blackhouse, on the Diamond Stanley-Durham service. One firm that remained by itself was the Langley Park Motor Co, which ran into Durham from that village and, in the late 1920s also a little further out from Quebec. Competition here seems to have been only from the North Eastern Railway and some occasional outsiders, both rejected by passengers, who stayed loyal to the village firm. The title by which the service was to be better known appeared first on an open charabanc of the period; *Gypsy Queen* was typical of the romantic names chosen in a drab time and place.

Since regular services had been instituted by those involved, there was little need for alteration by the commissioners after 1930. However, Northern also had an interest in several routes, and the result was co-ordinated timetables providing an even frequency. From Stanley to Quaking Houses and from Chester-le-Street to Grange Villa 15min services were achieved by Northern, alternating with Diamond and General respectively;

from Stanley to Durham Northern ran one journey of the four each hour. (These still apply today.) Changes of ownership took place within Diamond. As early as 1933 the members involved in Burnhope-Durham found it poor, and J. S. Mowbray took it over on condition that it was not shared. Before 1930 Mowbray had also run from Stanley to Burnhope, and from his experience thought it worth buying out the current operators Bainbridge and Dixon, provided again that he had sole rights. Others disposed of their shares, mainly to Mowbray (see Fig. 5) although when Mrs Hammel died her interest in Quaking Houses went to one son (W.) and in Durham to the other (J.H.). Finally W. Hammel sold his two shares in Quaking Houses to Mowbray, who thus became sole operator with Northern, while Mowbray and J. H. Hammel each acquired 50 per cent on the Durham route. To ensure fair shares the two businesses here exchange the schedules worked each week.

In the early post-war years difficulties in obtaining and maintaining buses led Mowbray to reduce his commitments. Traffic from Burnhope, a category D village, had never been good and in 1950 he gave up the service into Durham; it was taken over by Atkinson, who in 1946 had bought out Finlay and formed General Omnibus Services, a family partnership. For good measure General extended the Blackhouse route to Burnhope too.

Robert Armstrong of Ebchester, after selling his Majestic coach business to United (Chapter 4), had built up a haulage business, but in 1937 returned to passenger work by buying from Cowling's Motor Services a local route from Consett to the Hat and Feather which was run jointly with Venture. He expanded his coach fleet and then, in 1952, replaced Mowbray on the Stanley-Burnhope service for which, surprisingly, he opened a new garage at Annfield Plain. General meanwhile was beginning to regret becoming involved in Burnhope; in 1956 the Chester-le-Street route was cut back to Blackhouse again and Durham sold to S. R. Tyman (County Coaches) who abandoned it without warning at the end of the year. After a public inquiry at which witnesses declared the service to be 'of vital importance to the welfare of the village', Burn and Farrey (Kingsway) of Langley Park tried it for a month in 1958, and found six regular passengers. The route was now becoming notorious. Among others Tyman returned for a fortnight,

General for a little longer, and Richard Hardie of Chester-le-Street ran for a year in 1962–3. Finally, Armstrong took on the Saturday service in September 1963, although over the years he reduced it to two-hourly in summer only. J. H. Hammel and Mowbray provided a single weekday morning journey into Durham, returning in the evening – mainly to prevent others running over the route, which was largely common with Stanley-Durham, and merely diverting a bus which would have run into Durham anyway. The journey is operated by Hammel one week and by Mowbray the next.

One feels that the Burnhope saga is still not over. General decided to try extending the Blackhouse route once more in July 1973; when, predictably, it was found unrewarding, there was the possibility of a local authority subsidy, but this was refused. A year later Armstrong (now Robert jnr, son of the founder), closed the Annfield Plain garage and passed both Burnhope routes to Robert Fulton of Sacriston, a newcomer to bus work.

Thus in the mid 1970s independents are still important. The two largest firms, General and Mowbray, with 24 and 16 vehicles respectively, are heavily involved in schools and works contracts which have traditionally remained outside the associations. The smaller businesses such as Armstrong, now with seven and Gypsy Queen with six, concentrate on 'cleaner' work (Armstrong carries Coal Board clerical staff on contract but not miners) and maintain high standards of appearance. None has ever run double-deckers, and over the years motley second-hand fleets have given way to new; the extreme is Gypsy Queen, which needs two buses to run its basic service and replaces one each year.

South Durham

The topography changes south of Durham. Generally the mining villages are smaller and more scattered, with farming land between, and this seems to have led to a different pattern of bus services. Rather than running from village to town, many connect the major towns of the area, but follow devious routes to serve the mining communities. They overlap considerably in the central area around Ferryhill, a fact which has led to many disputes between operators in 'this very difficult area', as one traffic commissioner described it. Nor have they favoured large

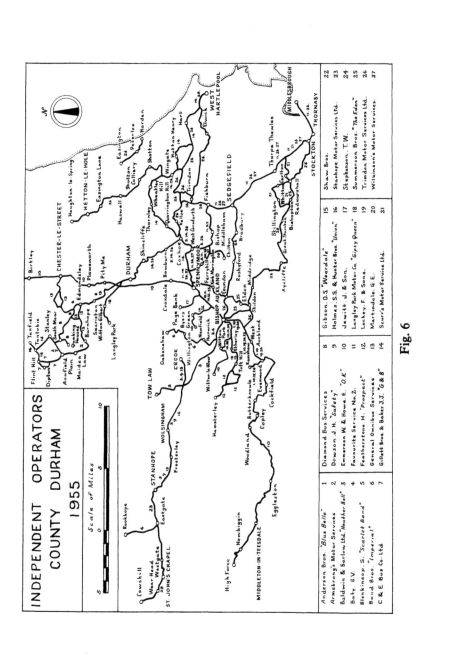

Fig. 6

associations, preferring rivalry – especially around Bishop Auckland, which is the equivalent of Stanley in being surrounded by a cluster of pit villages, and is also the centre for a large agricultural area.

The oldest surviving business is now the largest – that of Wade Emmerson, who began his Gaunless Valley Motor Service in 1912, running from Evenwood to Bishop Auckland or Darlington. After 1918 the business expanded, but began to experience competition from new operators; feeling that something 'more peppy' was needed by way of trading names, he remembered the American troops with whom he had served during the war, and chose 'OK'.

Many of the new busmen became so through adversity. The miners' strike of 1921 brought on the road the Gillett brothers (A. and A. H.) of Quarrington Hill, at first running casually to Thornley or Durham, and Stanley Blenkinsop in nearby West Cornforth who bought his first bus, a Fiat, for £410; he, too, ran into Durham using the 'Scarlet Band' title. The 1926 strike brought the Gilletts into full-time operation, linking Hartlepool with Durham and, soon after, Bishop Auckland. Needing more buses for this than they could afford, they joined forces at first with 'The Unity', a co-operative of Spennymoor owner-drivers, but they soon fell out among themselves and a long-standing association was formed with J. J. Baker. While the front of Blenkinsop buses showed a punning 'SB', Gillett and Baker displayed 'G&B'. Among those who started on OK's doorstep were Fred Lockey, a collier/shopkeeper/dealer and George Summerson, sometime United fitter, who first worked to Bishop from West Auckland in 1926/27. The Summersons lived next to the *Eden Arms* pub, named after the landowning family in West Auckland, hence The Eden Bus Service.

Also in 1927 Gordon Martindale lost his job as a cinema projectionist and bill-sticker in Ferryhill. For a month he drove on an important new venture, a route from Bishop Auckland to Newcastle, skirting the edge of Durham and needing three buses; one each was provided by 'A1', Emmerson, and E. Howe of Spennymoor. After running from Durham to Stockton for a time, Blenkinsop became involved in the A1, but on finding that his driver made regular detours to visit a lady-friend off the route he pulled out, leaving OK and Howe to share the service. Martindale meanwhile worked with W. Duffield, who was extending a Ferryhill local route to Stockton; from him he purchased a bus to run his own service to Ferryhill Station, a separate community, while Duffield's route eventually ran through from Stockton to Bishop Auckland.

Competition was now at its height. At West Auckland Lockey waited for the OK to come into view from Evenwood, then set off in front; at the other end the terminus was next to the cinema, and crews literally fought for passengers as they came out. The common enemy was United, with far greater resources; Lockey's response to the big company's 'flooding the road' was to advertise 'a penny all the way', while an OK and a United driver who had raced each other were once found with knives at each other's throats. When the Bond brothers of Willington began running to nearby Crook in 1922, United kept a bus permanently on the terminal stand; Bond's man would drive away (a bait to which the United driver rose) only to return round the block.

But this could not go on for ever. By 1925 the Bonds, under the 'Imperial' name, were running into Bishop Auckland jointly with E. Clark (Royal Bus Service), and Chamberlain Bros ('Elite'). Blenkinsop's principal rival on the Cornforth–Durham route was County Motors (Pearson and Johnson) who, like, Lockey, would wait at the bottom of Coxhoe Bank until the Scarlet Band came into sight. After receiving 14 summonses for running into Durham without a local authority licence, Blenkinsop curtailed his service at the nearest convenient point outside, thereafter running from Bowburn to Ferryhill Station. United also employed 'chasers' as a deterrent to Blenkinsop, one conductor being killed when he fell out of the back of his bus. He had been making faces at the driver of the inferior Scarlet Band vehicle being overtaken.

The Road Traffic Act was designed for areas like South Durham. Commissioners generally bestowed licences on those who could give evidence of regular operation, which meant in many cases shared routes. The first chairman of the commissioners made most services run at hourly intervals to simplify matters, and in many cases the resulting timetables are still used; even a 5min alteration might mean upsetting a rival somewhere along the route by being 2mins in front instead of 3mins behind. In practice one suspects that pre-1930 rivalry to keep just in front persists. The table below shows, in the example of Bishop Auckland–Spennymoor, how many operators and how great a frequency there might be on a partly country route; the timetable has not changed since before the war.

Departures from Bishop Auckland	Arrive Spennymoor	Operator	Destination
minutes past each hour			
00	15	United/NGT	Newcastle (56)
15	30	United/NGT/SDO	Sunderland (57)
20	37	Gillett/Baker	Hartlepool
30	45	United/NGT	Newcastle (56)
40	55	OK (Emerson/ Howe)	Newcastle
45	00	United/NGT/SDO	Sunderland (57)
50	05	Favourite No. 2 (Duffield, Potts, Roucroft)	Stockton

On the Evenwood route, licences were given to five operators, Emmerson, Lockey and Summerson, together with Anderson Bros of Evenwood and Stephenson Bros of High Etherley. However, Summerson was given only half of a 25 per cent share with Lockey, and decided to concentrate his attention on the uncontested West Auckland-Spennymoor route he had begun in 1928. Bishop Auckland lies at the southernmost point of a loop in the River Wear, after it leaves the Dale uplands; this was another very competitive area, with a market centre at Stanhope. Licences from this town to Crook were given to O. S. Gibson's Weardale Motor Services and J. Dowson ('Safety'), both of Frosterley, and to Baldwin and Barlow ('Heather Bell') of Tow Law, who also ran Stanhope–Bishop Auckland. Links between Weardale and B&B were to be strengthened in 1939, when they shared the southern half of a Consett–Tow Law–Stanhope route, with Northern taking the Consett end. West of Stanhope, a Mr Huntly acquired the businesses of Forrest and Stockdale, who ran to the head of the dale at Cowshill, and formed Stanhope Motor Services.

The more vigorous operators were now expanding. Emmerson purchased three businesses in the 1930s , in 1934 H. Rawe's 'Osborne Service' from Toft Hill, in 1936 J. Storey from Witton Park, and in 1939 F. Goundry from Newfield; all ran into Bishop Auckland, where a new headquarters and garage was opened in 1938. A couple of coaches remained at

154

Evenwood, though now they are kept for contract work. Emmerson's equivalent on the eastern side of the county was perhaps Trimdon Motor Services, which had become a limited company in 1929. The name had already been used since 1926 for an association between J. S. Grundy on one hand, and R. Paul and J. W. Seymour on the other; routes operated at the time were locally from Trimdon to Wingate (later extended to Houghton-le-Spring), and Durham–Trimdon–Hartlepool. Then, in 1935, Trimdon purchased Blenkinsop's old rival, County Motor Services, whose Durham–Ferryhill Station route was common with its own as far as Coxhoe.

The war years 1939–45 was a good period for the principal firms, despite reductions in the regular services. Emmerson increased his fleet to a maximum total of 70; this was partly for continuing traffic to Catterick Camp, an important source of revenue for both OK and United, while the building and manning of airfields at Dishforth, Leeming and Barnard Castle was useful too. Lockey also had contract work to Catterick, Trimdon to the Royal Ordnance Factory at Spennymoor, and Lockey, Summerson and Trimdon all carried workers to the Royal Ordnance Factory at Aycliffe. Indeed this wartime traffic pointed the way for post-war trends; Lockey was to concentrate on works contracts, while Summerson saw the traffic potential of the New Town that was being built on the factory site at Aycliffe. He turned the workers' journeys and an existing service into a regular Shildon-Aycliffe route in 1948 and later brought it into Bishop Auckland. The post-war traffic boom also introduced the first double-deckers to the independent fleets; Lockey and OK bought second-hand Leylands, a surviving tradition in both, while Weardale in 1949 bought a Leyland Titan too, but in this case a new one.

In 1929 Emmerson had started a route from Bishop Auckland to Woodland, later extended to Middleton-in-Teesdale and High Force leading to an interest in the Teesdale area generally. In the winter of 1947 a bus was snowbound at Middleton for some time, and local pressure for improved services into Barnard Castle led to a campaign in the *Teesdale Mercury* which accused OK of not caring for its passengers' welfare. Emmerson, a strong-minded man, could not tolerate such aspersions: he took legal action against the *Mercury*, and won, using as evidence a film of the first bus going through the snowdrift. This most rural of OK's activities only survived until 1963, then being cut back to Woodland once more.

Summerson continued his wise policy, in view of the number of category D villages around Bishop Auckland, of developing in Newton Aycliffe. This was not easy in view of United's similar interest, but workers' services were built up from surrounding villages and the Bishop Auckland route adapted to incorporate a local circular in the New Town; an Eden service from Aycliffe to Stockton also began in 1950 to take residents to a major shopping centre.

Trimdon Motor Services realised the similar possibilities of the other New Town in the area at Peterlee. A change of ownership in mid-1953 came in the middle of three important acquisitions. On 1 May, Alton Brothers of Trimdon and Taylor's Direct Services (Bishop Auckland) Ltd came into the fold; the first ran from Sedgefield to Hartlepool and from Ferryhill Station to Spennymoor, while the second had a short route from Bishop Auckland to Stockton (hence known as the Favourite Direct, by comparison with Duffield's longer route, now controlled by Harwood, which was the Favourite No 2). Finally, in November, Trimdon purchased J. W. Stewart of Horden, who two years earlier had pioneered local services in Peterlee. The nearby Houghton route was diverted to serve the Peterlee estates, but with the town growing more slowly than intended Trimdon found the Stewart routes unrewarding. They were taken over by United, a decision later regretted. In 1959 the business was sold again, to R. Lewis, a man described once as having a Midas touch. He changed a policy of buying second-hand buses, including double-deckers, to one of new single-deckers, kept for about five years, and the first Fords bought under this policy turned the corner for the company.

In 1962 the Houghton route was extended to Sedgefield and TMS, observing the strong links between the two New Towns, sought to take it further, into Aycliffe. This particular battle was won by United, which instead was allowed to divert an existing DDS route through Peterlee into Aycliffe, but as part of the deal a useful detour was allowed on the Direct — now known as Transport Motor Services, perhaps to correspond with the colloquially-used initials of Trimdon. Simultaneously Martindale extended his route in the same area to a new estate at Windlestone.

156

Lewis did not allow the grass to grow under his feet. When in 1966 the steelworks at Hartlepool set out to attract shift labour from the pit villages, the worthwhile contract for their transport was added to Trimdon's existing workers' traffic. Having lost Wilkinson's business to United in 1967, TMS secured Harwood's Favourite No 2 a month later (chapter 1) and in 1969 the remainder of Scurr's business in Stillington, involving a route into Stockton. Interestingly, Scurr's was latterly owned by Reginald Thompson, the brother of Gordon Thompson who controlled Wilkinson's. Lewis now turned his attention away from the North East; by 1973 his interests included Jersey Motor Transport, Heaps and Rogers Tours of Leeds, Norfolk Motor Services of Yarmouth and Granville Tours of Grimsby, making one of the largest independent groupings. All these companies adopted the blue and cream livery which had, except for a period around 1950, been used by Trimdon since the 1920s, together with a common glowing sun motif and the title 'Sunrise Tours' – perhaps not appropriate for Thornley in November.

The trend in the post-war years was strongly towards local monopolies. The three operators on the Willington-Bishop Auckland road were reduced to two in 1946 when Bond and F. Wilson, who had replaced Clark, bought out Chamberlain, and nine years later Bond had it to himself; this enabled him to continue his policy of running the Bishop Auckland journeys through to estates on the edge of Willington. O. S. Gibson in the same year purchased Stanhope Motor Services and, in March 1962, both Dawson's and Baldwin & Barlow's businesses, giving him a monopoly west of Crook. Although SMS remained as a separate company, and its garage was kept, in practice the two were regarded as one. Among the reasons for Stanhope and B&B selling was their willingness to run extra journeys after the Weardale railway passenger service closed, which brought little extra traffic, but substantial local objections later to the removal of the journeys.

Meanwhile, in 1959, the 'G&B' on Gillett and Baker buses gave way to 'GB' when Gillett Bros became sole operator, and in the following year OK moved rapidly towards a monopoly west of Bishop Auckland. January 1960 gave Emmerson half of the Evenwood route with the departure of Anderson Bros, which was increased to three-quarters in 1970 when Stephenson

Bros gave up. A Bishop Auckland town service began in 1962, followed a year later by the purchase of J. Featherstone, whose 'Prospect Service' ran to High Etherley and Hamsterley. Finally, E. Howe, who had also traded as 'OK', retired in 1968; as at Stanhope, the Spennymoor depot and company remained in existence, principally to run to Newcastle. All this activity might have been in vain, for Wade Emmerson died in 1969. Always a very secretive man, and with strong anti-trade union views, he had not confided even in his son Wade jnr who now became managing director. After a period of indecision C. S. Marshall was appointed personal assistant to Emmerson jnr and OK moved forward once more.

In the 1970s, the independents generally enjoy considerable public support and are in a strong position. Rivalry, though remaining, is tempered by co-operation to further common interests; an example was that the small band of Gillett and Trimdon inspectors checked each other's buses. On the other hand, Evenwood still rears its head in 1979. In the early days alternate journeys had been shortened at the country end, but to give each of the four operators a fair share it was agreed that the shortened journeys should be changed each week. Now that OK ran three of the four hourly departures it seemed sensible to stabilise the timetable, but Lockey declined. The effect is that Lockey runs the full route in alternate weeks only, and that passengers at the Ramshaw terminus have an hourly service one week, and half-hourly the next!

The two largest businesses are OK and Trimdon, with 50 or more vehicles each. Both have policies of generally running new fleets for a few years and at least partly using luxury coaches on bus work, especially where they compete with United; OK has also diversified into the holiday business, with a subsidiary 'OK Travel' agency company and a stake in the Northumbrian tourist trade.

Of the smaller businesses, perhaps the most impressive is Weardale/Stanhope, now controlled by O. S. Gibson's sons Maurice and Roland, with 20 vehicles. Since 1954 three-day trips to London, and eight-day seaside holidays have been run, which were followed in 1967 by senior citizens tours to Bournemouth and Torquay – all unusual in such a firm. One of its services, grant-aided by Durham County Council, is a single journey twice a week from Stanhope to Crawleyside, on the

Consett route abandoned by Venture; residents are apparently prepared to walk down into Stanhope but not to return uphill with their shopping. That business generally is good is suggested by the fact that, while OK has the largest capacity double-deckers in the North East – 83 seat Leyland Atlanteans – Weardale has the largest coaches, with 68 seats. Especially popular is a regular excursion to Newcastle, which frequently requires an Atlantean to convey its load of Weardale housewives.

Mid Northumberland

The independent stronghold has always been the area north of Hexham and west of Morpeth, not – as in Durham – because traffic was plentiful, but rather the reverse; United was never seriously interested. It includes much of Hadrian's Wall, a 400 square mile National Park with a population of 23,000 cattle, 303,000 sheep, and 2,000 people, and now large tracts of forestry plantations. It is an area attracting tourists appreciating wide open spaces, but by definition of little use to the bus operator. There are four principal lines of communication. One, the A68 from Scotch Corner to the Scottish border at Carter Bar, significantly has never had a regular bus service north of Consett; the A696, which links Newcastle with the A68 near Otterburn, carries the only United service, an infrequent Newcastle–Scottish route; and finally the North Tyne and Wansbeck Valleys upstream from Hexham and Morpeth. Despite these distinct routes, there have been many changes of ownership over the years involving the whole territory, and it is best to adopt a mainly chronological sequence.

The pioneer on the A696 was Robert Tait of Knowesgate, who in 1922 left his secure driving job with the County Council to run lorries, and a bus into Morpeth on Wednesdays and to Newcastle on Saturdays; by 1925 he had a second Morpeth route and was running daily to Newcastle. Before the Road Traffic Act, with a fleet of about six, a Hexham and a third Morpeth market bus were added, and by 1933 there was a fourth, but others were on the scene. Joseph Foster of Otterburn was making the long haul to Newcastle over various routes, including the direct one which competed with Tait, and E. Marshall was operating between Hexham and Morpeth. Services

TAIT'S DAILY BUS SERVICES

NEWCASTLE, BELSAY, CAPHEATON, KNOWESGATE

Phone Kirkwhelpington 25

	WEEKDAYS.			Sat.		SUNS.					WEEKDAYS.					SUNS.		
	a.m	p.m	p.m	p.m	p.m	p.m	p.m	p.m			a.m	a.m	p.m	p.m	p.m	p.m	p.m	p.m
NEWCASTLE (Haymarket)	9 30	2 15	5 30	8 45	10 0	2 15	9 30	10 0	KNOWESGATE	7 55	10 50	3 50	7 20	0	0 1	0 7	20
Ponteland	9 48	2 33	5 48	9 3	10 18	2 33	9 48	10 18	Kirkwhelpington		10 53	3 53				3	
Dissington Road End	9 50	2 35	5 50	9 5	10 20	2 35	9 50	10 20	Kirkharle Road End		11 0	4 0				10	
Higham Dykes	9 55	2 40	5 55	9 10	10 25	2 40	9 55	10 25	Capheaton Village		11 10	4 10				20	
Milbourne Road End	9 57	2 42	5 57	9 12	10 27	2 42	9 57	10 27	Harnham		11 20	4 20				25	
Belsay	10 5	2 50	6 5	9 20	10 35	2 50	10 5	10 35	Belsay	8 25	11 25	4 25	7 55	3 0	1 3	0 7	55
Harnham		2 55		9 25	10 40	2 55		10 40	Milbourne Road End	8 33	11 33	4 33	8 3	3	3 5	3 5	
Capheaton Village		3 5		9 35		3 5			Higham Dykes	8 35	11 35	4 35	8 5	4 5	4 5	8 5	
Kirkharle Road End		3 15		9 45	10 50	3 15		10 50	Dissington Road End	8 40	11 40	4 40	8 10	5 0	5 0	8 10	
Kirkwhelpington		3 20		9 53	10 55	3 20		10 55	Ponteland	8 42	11 42	4 42	8 12	5 2	5 2	8 12	
KNOWESGATE	10 40	3 25	6 40	9 55	11 0	3 25	10 40	11 0	NEWCASTLE	9 0	12 0	5 0	8 30	2 10	2 10	8 30	

NEWCASTLE, BELSAY, CAMBO, KNOWESGATE

	WEEKDAYS.			Sat.		SUNS.					WEEKDAYS.					SUNS.	
	a.m	p.m	p.m	p.m	p.m	p.m	p.m	p.m			a.m	a.m	p.m	p.m	p.m	p.m	p.m
NEWCASTLE (Haymarket)	9 30	2 15	5 30	8 45	10 0	2 15	9 30	10 0	KNOWESGATE	7 55	10 50	3 50	7 20	0	0 1	0 7 20
Ponteland	9 48	2 33	5 48	9 3	10 18	2 33	9 48	10 18	Hartington Road End	7 58			7 24	1		7 24
Dissington Road End	9 50	2 35	5 50	9 5	10 20	2 35	9 50	10 20	Cambo	8 5			7 30	1 10		7 30
Higham Dykes	9 55	2 40	5 55	9 10	10 25	2 40	9 55	10 25	Wellington	8 8			7 33	1 13		7 33
Milbourne Road End	9 57	2 42	5 57	9 12	10 27	2 42	9 57	10 27	Middleton Bridge	8 12			7 38	1 18		7 38
Belsay	10 5	2 50	6 5	9 20	10 35	2 50	10 5	10 35	Bolam West House	8 15			7 42	1 22		7 42
Bolam Bogg	10 12		6 12			2 55	10 12		Bolam Bogg	8 18			7 45	1 25		7 45
Bolam West House	10 15		6 15			3 0	10 15		Belsay	8 25	11 25	4 25	7 55	3 0	1 36	3 6 7 55
Middleton Bridge	10 20		6 20			3 5	10 20		Milbourne Road End	8 33	11 33	4 33	8 3	3	4 3	4 3 8 3
Wellington	10 25		6 25			3 10	10 25		Higham Dykes	8 35	11 35	4 35	8 5	4 5	4 5	8 5
Cambo	10 30		6 30			3 15	10 30		Dissington Road End	8 40	11 40	4 40	8 10	5 0	5 0	8 10
Hartington Road End	10 35		6 35			3 20	10 35		Ponteland	8 42	11 42	4 42	8 12	5 2	5 2	8 12
KNOWESGATE	10 40	3 25	6 40	9 55	11 0	3 25	10 40	11 0	NEWCASTLE	9 0	12 0	5 0	8 30	2 10	2 10	8 30

MORPETH, LONGWITTON, KNOWESGATE

	WEEKDAYS.				SUNS.					WEEKDAYS.				SUNS.
	a.m	p.m	w	p.m		p.m	p.m			a.m	p.m	p.m	w	p.m	p.m
MORPETH (New Market)	10 30	2 30	6 30	9 0		2 30	9 0	KNOWESGATE	8 30	12 30	5 0	7 30	1 0 6 0
Benridge	10 40	2 40	6 40	9 10		2 40	9 10	Hartington	8 35	12 35	5 5	7 35	5 6 5
Pigdon	10 45	2 45	6 45	9 15		2 45	9 15	Rothley	8 45	12 45	5 15	7 45	15 6 15
Netherwitton	10 55	2 55	6 55	9 25		2 55	9 25	Longwitton	8 50	12 50	5 20	7 50	20 6 20
Longwitton	11 5	3 5	7 5	9 35		3 5	9 35	Netherwitton	9 0	1 0	5 30	8 0	30 6 30
Rothley	11 10	3 10	7 10	9 40		3 10	9 40	Pigdon	9 10	1 10	5 40	8 10	40 6 40
Hartington	11 20	3 20	7 20	9 50		3 20	9 50	Benridge	9 15	1 15	5 45	8 15	45 6 45
KNOWESGATE	11 25	3 25	7 25	9 55		3 25	9 55	MORPETH	9 25	1 25	5 55	8 25	55 6 55

w Weds. and Sats.

Fig. 7

JOSEPH FOSTER & SON

Phone
Otterburn 27

NEWCASTLE, HUMSHAUGH, CHOLLERFORD, WARK, BELLINGHAM

NEWCASTLE	Mon. to Fri.		Saturday	Sunday			Mon. to Fri.		Saturday	Sunday
	am	pm	am pm pm	pm pm			am pm		am pm pm	pm pm
NEWCASTLE (Haymarket)	11 0	6 15	11 0 3 30 6 15	3 15 9 0		OTTERBURN	7 30 3 45		7 30	1 0 6 30
Lemington Rd. E.	11 12	6 27	11 12 3 42 6 27	3 27 9 12		Hareshaw	7 45 4 0		7 45	1 15 6 45
Blucher	11 14	6 29	11 14 3 44 6 29	3 29 9 14		Tarset	8 e 0			
Walbottle	11 16	6 31	11 16 3 46 6 31	3 31 9 16		Bellingham	8 15 4 15		8 15 12 45 4 15	1 30 7 0
Throckley	11 19	6 34	11 19 3 49 6 34	3 34 9 19		Wark	8 30 4 30		8 30 1 0 4 30	1 45 7 15
Heddon	11 22	6 37	11 22 3 52 6 37	3 37 9 22		Nunwick	8 32 4 32		8 32 1 2 4 32	1 47 7 17
Harlow Hill	11 30	6 45	11 30 3 0 6 45	3 45 9 30		Humshaugh—Chollerford	8 44 4 44		8 44 1 14 4 44	1 59 7 29
Whittle Dene	11 31	6 46	11 31 3 1 6 46	3 46 9 31		St. Oswald's	8 54 4 54		8 54 1 24 4 54	2 9 7 39
Halton Shield	11 40	6 55	11 40 3 10 6 55	3 55 9 40		Stagsh'wb'k Gate	8 59 4 59		8 59 1 29 4 59	2 14 7 44
Stagsh'wb'k Gate	11 45	7 0	11 45 3 15 7 0	0 9 45		Halton Shield	9 3 5 3		9 3 1 32 5 3	2 18 7 48
St. Oswald's	11 51	7 6	11 51 3 20 7 5	5 9 51		Whittle Dene	9 15 5 15		9 15 1 45 5 15	2 30 8 0
Chollerford—Humshaugh	12 07	15	12 0 3 30 7 15	4 15 10 0		Harlow Hill	9 16 5 16		9 16 1 46 5 16	2 31 8 1
						Heddon	9 24 5 24		9 24 1 54 5 24	2 39 8 9
Fenwick	12 12	7 27	12 12 3 42 7 27	4 27 10 12		Throckley	9 27 5 27		9 27 1 57 5 27	2 42 8 12
Wark	12 15	7 30	12 15 3 44 7 30	4 30 10 15		Walbottle	9 30 5 30		9 30 2 0 5 30	2 45 8 15
Bellingham	12 30	7 50	12 30 4 0 7 45	4 45 10 30		Blucher	9 32 5 32		9 32 2 2 5 32	2 47 8 17
Tarset		8 e 0				Lemington Rd. E.	9 34 5 34		9 34 2 4 5 34	2 49 8 19
Hareshaw	12 45	8 5	8 5	5 5 10 40		NEWCASTLE	9 45 5 45		9 45 2 15 5 45	3 0 8 30
OTTERBURN	1 0	8 20	8 20	5 20 10 50						

OTTERBURN, KIRKWHELPINGTON, BELSAY, NEWCASTLE

	Mondays to Fridays		Saturdays	Suns.			Mons. to Fris.		Saturdays	Suns.
	a.m. am pm pm		am pm pm pm	pm pm pm			a.m pm pm pm		am N'n pm pm pm pm	pm pm
NEWCASTLE	10 0 6 0 9 10		10 0	2 0 6 0 9 10	2 30 9 10	Rochester	7 0 45		12 10	
Ponteland	10 18 6 18 9 28		10 18	2 18 6 18 9 28	2 48 9 28	OTTERBURN	8 0 12 30 6 30		8 0 12 0 12 30 6 30	1 0 6 30
Dissing't Rd. E'd	10 20 6 20 9 30		10 20	2 20 6 20 9 30	2 50 9 30	Cross Ho. Rd. End	8 2 12 32 6 32		8 2 12 2 12 32 6 32	2 6 32
Higham Dykes	10 25 6 25 9 35		10 25	2 25 6 25 9 35	2 55 9 35	Elsdon	8 6 7		8 7 12 10	
Milbourne Rd. E.	10 27 6 27 9 37		10 27	2 27 6 27 9 37	2 57 9 37	Cross Ho. Rd. End				
Highlander	10 31 6 31 9 41		10 31	2 31 6 31 9 41	3 1 9 41	Monkridge	12 34 6 34		12 34 6 34	4 6 34
Belsay	10 35 6 35 9 45		10 35	2 35 6 35 9 45	5 9 45	Blaxter	8 19 12 40 6 40	8 19	12 40 6 40	1 0 6 40
Capheaton Rd. E.	10 47 6 47 9 57		10 47	2 47 6 47 9 57	3 17 9 57	Knowegate	8 35 12 50 6 50	8 35	12 50 6 50	
Kirkwhelpington	10 57 6 57 10 7		10 57	2 57 6 57 10 7	3 27 10 7	Kirkwhelpington	8 38 12 53 6 53	8 38	12 53 6 53	2 36 53
Knowegate	11 0 7 0 10 10		11 0	3 0 7 0 10 10	3 30 10 10	Capheaton Rd. E.	8 48 1 3 7 3	8 48	1 3 7 3	3 3 3 7 3
Blaxter	11 10 7 10 10 20		11 10	3 10 7 10 10 20	3 40 10 20	Belsay	9 0 1 15 7 15	9 0	1 15 7 15	4 5 7 15
Monkridge	11 16		11 16	3 16	3 46	Highlander	9 4 1 19 7 19	9 4	1 19 7 19	4 9 7 19
Cross Ho. Rd. End	11 18		11 18	3 18	3 48	Millourne Rd. E'd	9 8 1 23 7 23	9 8	1 23 7 23	4 5 7 23
Elsdon	7 0 25 10 35 d		12 20	7 25 10 35 c	10 35 c	Higham Dykes	9 10 1 25 7 25	9 10	1 25 7 25	5 5 7 25
Cross Ho. Rd. End	7 33 10 43		12 32	7 33 10 43	10 43	Dissing'n Rd. E'd	9 15 1 30 7 30	9 15	1 30 7 30	0 7 30
OTTERBURN	7 0 30 12 07 35 10 45		11 20	3 20 7 35 10 45 50 10 45		Ponteland	9 17 1 32 7 32	9 17	1 32 7 32	2 7 32
Rochester	7 0 45 a 7 55		11 40	7 55	11 0	NEWCASTLE	9 35 1 50 7 50	9 35	1 50 7 50	2 20 7 50

NEWCASTLE, BARRASFORD, WOODBURN, OTTERBURN

	Mons. to Fris.		Saturdays	Sundays			Mons. to Fris.		Saturdays	Sundays
	am pm		am pm	pm pm			am pm		am pm	pm pm
NEWCASTLE (Haymarket) dep	10 15 6 15		10 15 6 15	3 30 9 0		OTTERBURN dep	7 40 3 40		7 40	0 6 10
Whorlton (Church)	10 31 6 31		10 31 6 31	3 46 9 16		Woodburn	8 0 4 0		8 0 12 30	20 6 30
Callerton	10 36 6 36		10 36 6 36	3 51 9 21		Ridsdale	8 6 4 6		8 6 12 36	26 6 36
Birney Estate	10 40 6 40		10 40 6 40	3 55 9 25		Tone Inn	8 14 4 14		8 14 12 44	34 6 44
Plough Inn	10 43 6 43		10 43 6 43	3 58 9 28		Coltcrag	8 17 4 17		8 17 12 47	37 6 47
Stamfordham	10 51 6 51		10 51 6 51	4 6 9 36		Barrasford San.	8 22 4 22		8 22 12 52	42 6 52
Fenwick	10 57 6 57		10 57 6 57	4 12 9 42		Gunnerton	8 29 4 29		8 29 12 59	49 6 59
Matfen	11 1 7 1		11 1 7 1	4 16 9 46		Barrasford	8 34 4 34		8 34 1 4	54 7 4
Great Whittington	11 6 7 6		11 6 7 6	4 21 9 51		Chollerton	8 37 4 37		8 37 1 7	5 7 7 7
Whittington Rd. End	11 9 7 9		11 9 7 9	4 24 9 54		Swinburn Lodge	8 41 4 41		8 41 1 11	1 7 11
Halton Red House	11 9 7 9		11 9 7 9	4 24 9 54		Colwell	8 46 4 46		8 46 1 16	6 7 16
Stagshawbank Gate	11 10 7 10		11 10 7 10	4 25 9 55		Five Lane Ends	8 47 4 47		8 47 1 17	7 7 17
Bingfield	11 18 7 18		11 18 7 18	4 33 10 3		Bingfield	8 57 4 57		8 57 1 27	17 7 27
Five Lane Ends	11 28 7 28		11 28 7 28	4 43 10 13		Stagshawbank Gate	9 5 5		9 5 1 35	25 7 35
Colwell	11 29 7 29		11 29 7 29	4 44 10 14		Halton Red House	9 6 5 6		9 6 1 36	26 7 36
Swinburn Lodge	11 34 7 34		11 34 7 34	4 49 10 19		Whittington Rd. E'd	9 6 5 6		9 6 1 36	26 7 36
Chollerton	11 38 7 38		11 38 7 38	4 53 10 23		G. Whittington	9 9 5 9		9 9 1 39	29 7 39
Barrasford	11 41 7 41		11 41 7 41	4 56 10 26		Matfen	9 14 5 14		9 14 1 44	34 7 44
Gunnerton	11 46 7 46		11 46 7 46	1 10 31		Fenwick	9 18 5 18		9 18 1 48	38 7 48
Barrasford San.	11 53 7 53		11 53 7 53	8 10 38		Stamfordham	9 24 5 24		9 24 1 54	44 7 54
Coltcrag	11 58 7 58		11 58 7 58	5 13 10 43		Plough Inn	9 32 5 32		9 32 2 2	52 8 2
Tone Inn	12 1 8 1		12 1 8 1	5 16 10 46		Birney Estate	9 35 5 35		9 35 2 5	55 8 5
Ridsdale	12 9 8 9		12 9 8 9	5 24 10 54		Callerton	9 39 5 39		9 39 2 9	59 8 9
Woodburn	12 15 8 15		12 15 8 15	5 30 11 0		Whorlton (Church)	9 44 5 44		9 44 2 14	4 8 14
OTTERBURN	12 35 8 35		8 35	5 50 11 20		NEWCASTLE	10 0 6 0		10 0 2 30	20 8 30

a Tues., Thurs. b Mons., Thurs. & Sats. c If passengers. d Mons., Thurs. & Sats. if passengers. e Tarset, Thurs. only.
HEXHAM TO OTTERBURN, via Wall, Chollerton, Fourlaws, Ridsdale and West Woodburn.—Tuesdays, leave Hexham 4 20 pm.
Parcels : Marr's Shop, Haymarket. Tuesdays, leave Otterburn 8 0 am.
Light Luggage carried free, owner's risk. Parcels carried by all services at sender's risk.

Fig. 8

in the North Tyne Valley, from Newcastle and Hexham to Bellingham and thence to Kielder and Ridsdale, were provided from 1928 by Cecil Moffit, who before 1939 also acquired the Hexham–Wark and Colwell routes of W. Charlton; westwards from Hexham M. S. Charlton of Newbrough (no relation) had a brisk business. Beginning in 1919, he acquired a route from Hexham to Haydon Bridge from W. Wharton in 1934 which became the basis of his regular service.

Such was the pattern in 1945. Optimism about post-war prospects seems to have been greater in Northumberland and to have lasted longer than one would expect in such territory. A network of daily services came into existence reaching their peak in the mid 1950s possibly because job opportunities were not scattered throughout the countryside but concentrated in the main market towns, and the resulting development of strong links to a limited number of centres.

It may have been such thinking that induced Crown Coaches of Newcastle, a hitherto obscure organisation, to acquire rapidly in 1947 Foster's and Marshall's businesses, together with Tait's Newcastle and one Morpeth route and a service from Newcastle to RAF Ouston. This last had only recently been started by Robert Armstrong of Newcastle (again unconnected with his namesake at Ebchester), otherwise then purely a provider of contract buses. In 1944 Crown Coaches had purchased Bedlington & District Luxury Coaches, a firm dating back to 1923 which, apart from one local route, was again a contract operator. In 1947 the proprietors of B&D bought back their interest, although there had been and still was a strong family connection between the two. This business (which despite its name is based in Ashington and has no luxury coaches, but only second-hand buses) still exists as the largest Northumberland independent, and relies overwhelmingly on miners' traffic.

Crown soon realised its mistake. As early as 1949, a Foster route, now cut back to West Woodburn, passed to Moffit, and two years later G. Marshall, a member of the original family, formed a partnership with a Crown driver, Jack Rochester, to take back the Hexham–Morpeth run. A very old-established Newcastle operator, Galley's Coaches, then took over the remainder of Crown's routes in 1953, although its only previous experience of regular services had been a Newcastle–Hull express taken over by East Yorkshire before the war. Galley's went further, and collected back the West Woodburn route from Moffit, ambitiously trying also a once-weekly market run over the Border to Hawick.

Moffit at this time reduced his fleet from 15 vehicles to nine. In 1950 the routes north of Bellingham went to a local man, F. B. Rutherford, who later abandoned them; W. A. Charlton, the son of the original operator, took over his father's Wark and Colwell services in 1953.

Considering its population the area was well endowed with railway track, if not with many trains. The search for coal in the mid-19th century extended to Plashetts, high in the hills beyond Bellingham, where there was a small ironworks, and the rush to exploit Plashetts coal coincided with plans to evolve a

Tyneside–Scottish rail route outside the control of the North Eastern Railway. Thus the Border Counties Railway was opened west from Morpeth, which met a branch from Hexham at Redesmouth, meandered north-westwards through Bellingham to Plashetts, Kielder, and then crossed the border to join the Carlisle–Edinburgh Waverley route. John Thomas wrote 'The Border Counties met the Border Union on a bare hillside . . . Before the railways came there was nothing on the spot, the nearest public road being two miles away. The North British built a station in the wilderness and called it Riccarton Junction.' In practice the main uses to which the line was put were the carriage of livestock and of armaments to a testing site in the hills.

In 1956, the lines from Hexham to Riccarton and from Morpeth to Redesmouth were to be closed. As far as Bellingham there were adequate bus services, but not beyond; a replacement had to be provided and, if necessary, subsidised by British Railways, before the closure could take place. It was rumoured that £3,000 a year was given to Norman Fox of Falstone, who since Rutherford's departure had provided school buses north of Bellingham, to provide this facility. The then hard-pressed established operators felt that such a generous grant – Fox argued that the poor roads made his costs high – should have been given to one of them, probably Moffit. Since there was no road to Riccarton, Fox ran his service to the next station south at Steele Road, though never more than three days a week. Otherwise he terminated at Kielder, and after passengers were suitably discouraged by the railway custom of changing timetables to eliminate bus connections, all journeys were curtailed there. From this area, however, traffic actually increased as forestry spread over the hills and hamlets were built for employees. When Fox died in 1967 his route was taken over by H. Thompson, a garage proprietor in Bellingham with one or two coaches.

The railway from Redesmouth to Morpeth was partly covered by Tait's remaining services, but also by J. Batty, who in 1946 bought from J. Robson routes from Morpeth to Hexham and Scots Gap. A cousin, W. J. Batty, was proprietor of Wansbeck Motor Services of Ashington, one of the few remaining small operators in industrial Northumberland. In the 1950s both Batty and Tait reduced their services west of

164

Morpeth but Tait acquired a better proposition in a local route licenced to O. Merson, and in 1961 confirmed the business, now Morpeth-based, by taking on a Saturday run to Eshott which Batty had started earlier. Meanwhile it had been proved that traffic on the railway was not enough for the closure to do Batty any good when, in 1958, he announced his intention of abandoning the main service, partly the effect of depression at seeing intending passengers picked up by well-meaning neighbours' cars. A hasty public meeting was attended by United, the chairman of the commissioners, and Morpeth's MP, with the result that a United bus was made available to Batty, his fares were increased, and the business struggled on.

In Hexham, the number of operators was to fall sharply. Moffit disposed of the remainder of his business in 1958 to Jack Charlton, whose father's Newbrough business had expanded; two subsidiary companies, Passenger Transport (Gilsland) and Haltwhistle & District Miners Transport Services, were formed jointly with Sowerby's Tours of Gilsland for large-scale workers' transport. The latter speaks for itself, while the former was concerned with a rocket site at Spadeadam. At this stage, with 28 buses, a new company was formed in January 1961 as Mid-Tyne Transport Ltd, but after only nine months a receiver was called in. Remarkably the business proceeded the next year to take over W. A. Charlton's operation and then continued under the receiver until 1967.

Rochester and Marshall meanwhile expanded too. Like Crown, Galley's soon began to regret its country services and handed over the West Woodburn route yet again in 1955. A Galley driver, T. B. Vasey, took on the remainder but died soon afterwards; a year later his brother, C. O. Vasey, who was a Tyne shipbuilder, stepped into the breach. By 1962 he had had enough, and gave the Hexham route to Mid-Tyne, who after three months passed it on to R&M. The Newcastle service went to W. M. Appleby of Choppington, who (under a variety of trading names) since 1938 had been running between Newcastle and Morpeth, using the A696 as far as Belsay. Finally in 1967 T. B. Vasey's son and namesake, who had been driving for Appleby, took the service back while Appleby continued to run to Morpeth, then as 'Terrier Coaches' and later as 'Highway International'.

R&M began a Hexham town service in 1961 but probably

cancelled out this profitable work by taking over in 1963 the ailing business of C. R. Robson of Smelting Syke, whose routes south of Hexham towards Consett and Blanchland had been reduced. By the end of 1964 R&M could carry on the West Woodburn route no longer, but felt it necessary to attract public attention to its plight. The last bus sported black ribbons throughout the day, wreaths were placed on its bonnet at Newcastle, Great Whittington and Woodburn, and placards condemned the fuel tax which R&M felt added unnecessarily to its difficulties. Each passenger received a letter:

WOODBURN–NEWCASTLE
WITHDRAWAL OF BUS SERVICE
LAST DAY OF OPERATION
SUNDAY 20th DECEMBER 1964

The Directors regret that they are unable to subsidise the Woodburn–Newcastle service from other revenue for a further period. The service has been operated entirely at the company's expense for the last four years.

The current rate of fuel tax of 2s 9d plus 6d a gallon just does not make sense when imposed on a rural service of this kind. The Company has been paying in fuel tax on this service alone £290 per annum, which is almost identical with the loss that this route has been showing. The Company maintain that if fuel tax was not applied to rural services of this nature, then these routes would not have to be withdrawn, thereby depriving rural dwellers of public transport.

Rochester and Marshall Ltd has grown from a Company established in 1925 and now runs 15 vehicles on 13 stage services, most of which are operated on the proverbial shoestring, and the Company considers that if this punitive fuel tax continues more licences will have to be surrendered.

Almost ten years later the hated tax was finally removed, though only after a dramatic increase in the basic price of fuel.

Galley's meanwhile was purchased in 1960 by Armstrong, who in 1954 had recommenced bus operation by taking over from Bell's Services, a United subsidiary, a route from Newcastle to Stamfordham and villages in R&M territory. Also in 1960 Armstrong purchased a service with growth potential from central Newcastle to the airport at Woolsington, which built up over the years to a peak summer traffic of about 1,000 passengers a week; in 1964 Moor–Dale Coaches, once a North Riding bus operator but now mainly running school buses in Newcastle, came under Armstrong control. This was the nearest to a large independent coach business, surprisingly, that ever existed on Tyneside. Armstrong died in 1966 and three years later his nephew E. Dunn separated Moor–Dale again and bought Curtis of Dudley, a similar coach firm, while in 1973 after Mrs Armstrong's death the Armstrong and Galley fleets were sold to Tyneside PTE and, from April 1974, the Stamfordham route was worked by Slatyford drivers. Another similar route was added in September 1975 when Appleby ceased operating and the yellow buses ran into Morpeth for the first time.

This brings the story, rather a catalogue of disasters, nearly up to date and it might be expected that more was to come; but there is a happy ending. Northumberland County Council was unusually fortunate in having on its planning staff Douglas Mennear, who not only sympathised with the operators but knew them and their problems well. Northumberland was the first English county to give rural grants after 1968 and did more than simply retain the existing services. While R&M, Vasey, Appleby, Thompson and Batty received subsidies for their country routes, school buses have been granted 'section 30 permits' under the 1968 legislation, not only enabling them to carry ordinary passengers but permitting their owners to claim fuel tax rebate and Treasury aid in buying new buses. In one extreme case the county loaned Vasey the price of a new coach in 1972 which, being the first new vehicle to appear on his route for 20 years, had the desirable effect of increasing traffic by 20 per cent. Vasey was also encouraged by the county to restore once more a service between Newcastle, West Woodburn and Bellingham on a once-a-day basis, simply by making better use of a bus that was carrying children to and from school in Bellingham. Another novelty in 1974 was a tourist service connecting places of interest along Hadrian's Wall using R&M coaches in conjunction with United's Roman Wall route.

This interest on the council's part did not please everyone. Mid-Tyne passed in April 1967 from the receiver to Tyne Valley Coaches, a company formed by W. D. Sowerby and R. B. Hindmarsh, who became managing director. For a period Tyne

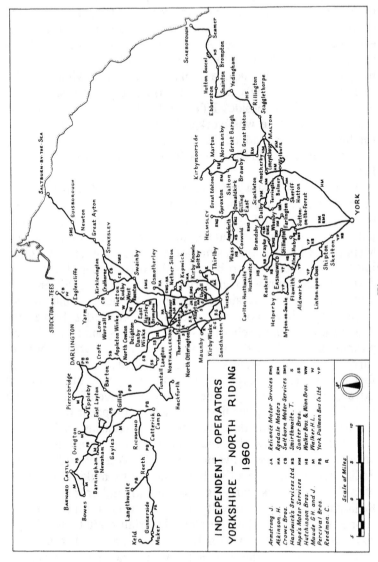

INDEPENDENT OPERATORS
YORKSHIRE – NORTH RIDING
1960

Armstrong J.	JA	Reliance Motor Services	RMS
Atkinson H.	HA	Ryedale Motors	RM
Crowe Bros.	CB	Saltburn Motor Services	SMS
Hardwick's Services Ltd	HS	Smirthwaite. T.	S
Hope's Motor Services	HM	Sunter Bros.	SB
Hutchinson Bros.	HB	Walker Bros. & Nunn Bros.	WW
Maude G H and J.	M	Walker H.L.	W
Percival Bros.	PB	York Pullman Bus (o)Ltd	YP
Reedman C.	R		

Scale of Miles

Fig. 9

Valley was subsidised too, but, after Sowerby dropped out in 1971, Hindmarsh preferred the alternative course of raising his fares, cutting out little-used journeys and looking for more profitable business. He increased his private hire and tour work, making a speciality of continental trips for local schools, and remains at a strength of 28 coaches the largest independent in the area. The differences between Tyne Valley and the County were eventually resolved with an agreement to subsidise poorly used journeys.

York and the North Riding

The area concerned is the Plain of York southwards from Northallerton to York. As rich agricultural land it resembles the southern part of Durham, but in the history of its buses it is more like Northumberland. The survival of independent businesses has often been associated with the boundary areas of the territorial companies; these were often drawn at natural traffic watersheds, which were not worth further colonisation, or were sometimes artificial, in which case routes on the edge might be difficult to fit into the network. Here we have a combination of the two, the whole forming the frontier between United, East Yorkshire and West Yorkshire.

The northern part, around Thirsk and Northallerton, has had a history of routes changing hands between overlapping small operators, who ran only a few journeys a week. Perhaps, along the East Coast main railway line, this was all that was necessary, but in the early 1960s when intermediate stations were closed, most bus routes were either abandoned or passed to new operators, the common sign of financial malaise. In 1960, for example, the fairly large firm of Percival Bros acquired two Northallerton routes from Sunter Bros, who then specialised in heavy haulage work; but by 1970 all that was left of Percival's business was the Swaledale route (chapter 1). The only independent to survive the decade was H. Atkinson of Ingleby, who curtailed his services to three market routes a week, while a newcomer, J. Smith of Dalton, from 1968 ran a reduced version of those previously operated by C. Reedman of Thirsk and T. Smirthwaite of Northallerton. These were to be subsidised by the North Riding County Council, although one might think it was rather too late.

169

One business to stay the course was Reliance Motor Services, founded in York by E. Sheriff in 1928. A basic two-hourly frequency between York and Helmsley, deviating from the direct north-south route to serve Easingwold and smaller communities, was the mainstay for nearly 40 years. However, after 1953 Sheriff was unable to afford new buses and, like Rochester and Marshall, was bitterly critical of the fuel tax. He then relied on older buses supplied by West Yorkshire, which also did his routine licensing work; United was another large company which, in the case of Fox and Batty, helped non-competitive independents in the same way. In 1966, the year Sheriff died, he found it necessary to truncate the route at Brandsby, abandoning nearly half. Councillors in Helmsley said: 'Reliance's years of service have been appreciated in Helmsley. Nothing short of 10ft snowdrifts prevented them from keeping the service going.' and 'Many of us can remember the wonderful job they did during the war years particularly. Throughout the whole time their efforts to serve the travelling public have gone beyond the normal call of duty.' Unfortunately these sentiments did not assist Reliance's finances. For a while a local minibus owner, D. Gray, maintained the Helmsley service by connecting at Brandsby, and after he gave up, West Yorkshire provided a York–Helmsley facility by extending a Malton route to Ampleforth and connecting there with United. This circuitous route was unlikely to attract many customers. Sheriff's daughter and son-in-law, R. Shelton, continue to run the York–Brandsby service, although reduced again to require a single bus.

Against this background the growth of a successful larger independent, especially one based in York, where West Yorkshire had a major depot, is remarkable. The city itself was always the dividing line between the East and West Yorkshire companies, and perhaps because of this and the fact that the country routes of both were poor, several independents have survived, but none in the same league as York Pullman.

Hartas Foxton was an accountant, from a well-known local farming family, who opened a garage in Piccadilly, York after the first world war; Foxton's Garage, now much larger and a Ford main dealer, is still there opposite Pullman's terminus. He started a Red Bus Service north from the city to Easingwold and in 1926 took over the 'Netta' business running in the same area from Messrs. Hutchinson and Greenland. These two were ex-

United employees among whose drivers was George Summerson; it was when he realised that Netta faced too much competition that he started his own Eden service in West Auckland. On the other side of York, another garage proprietor named Pierce secured assistance from Foxton with his 'Pullman' operation to Murton and Stamford Bridge. In October they formed the York Pullman Bus Company, which merged with Red Bus in 1930, after Pierce had handed over his share. The purchase of three more businesses in the next three years brought Pullman to a scale of operation which was to stay almost constant. First was R. P. and N. M. Walls, who ran from a base at Holme-on-Spalding-Moor to York, Market Weighton and Selby; then C. J. Wainwright, whose Wheldrake–York route was a shortened version of Walls', and lastly R. Whitehead, a York coach operator. Whitehead also had a taxi and funeral business which he kept for two years, when Pullman took that over too, but it was resold during the war.

In 1938, Pullman opened the garage that was needed to house the entire fleet in Navigation Road, York; the Offices were in Bootham Tower, a unique site in that they formed part of the medieval city wall. Pullman appeared to come to the conclusion that it had now reached an ideal size, in that no more bus operators were taken over. On the other hand, the Whitehead purchase was important in that it formed the basis of an excursion and tour business which grew substantially. Pullman had a near-monopoly in this field as, perhaps because of railway influence, no major express services started in the city, and it was the only centre from which West Yorkshire lacked excursion licences.

The bus routes fell naturally into two halves, those to the East Riding which started in Piccadilly, and those into the North Riding, which terminated at Exhibition Square (adjoining Bootham Tower). In the post-war years the East Riding side was that which gave problems, while to the north housing developments and an RAF station at Linton-on-Ouse led to growth. Thus, in 1953, the Murton short journeys were handed over to West Yorkshire and in 1954 Holme garage, which had been kept, was closed. The York route was maintained, but J. H. Thornes of Bubwith took over, and later abandoned, that to Market Weighton and the less frequent of the Selby pair. Thornes still runs the other Selby route and connects with

171

Pullman. On the other hand, the first three double-deckers were bought in 1954 and used mainly on the north side, while a housing estate at Skelton later required an extra service from the city.

Finally, in 1968 the small coach business of Fawcett of Acomb was purchased, which helped in the build-up of tour destinations during the 1960s. Hartas Foxton had died in 1960, the company continuing under the ownership of his nephews and nieces but managed by A. Graham, the company's accountant since 1930. One of Foxton's contributions was the establishment of regular shifts for the crews, in contrast to the practice of most companies where staff work different duties each day, and this helped to keep down the problem of labour turnover from which most industries in York suffer. Despite the increase in coach work, buses are still responsible for more than half the mileage run.

Overall the immaculate appearance of the Pullman vehicles in their yellow, maroon and cream, encouraged by each coach having its own driver, heightens the impression of the independent operator at his best. Although some of the bus routes now need to be subsidised, one feels there is much to be gained from the continuation of businesses like York Pullman, not only in the counties of the North East but elsewhere.

8

CONCLUSION

After a period of relative stability, the organisation of the bus industry in the North East seemed likely to change as this book was being completed. The directors of Scott's Greys acquired control of GNE Motor Services, while one of the most important Durham independents, Gillett Bros, was sold to United followed closely by Shaw Bros of Byers Green. Moor–Dale, by taking over the Rochester & Marshall business in 1975, seemed on the other hand to have confidence in the future of the medium-sized independent firm. In many ways, such as general standard of living and level of car ownership, the area is about ten years behind the United Kingdom as a whole, and one is tempted to suggest that this might be true of the bus industry also. In the 1960s there was a marked trend among independents to sell as the original proprietors reached retiring age or died; in the North they seem to have survived longer or, perhaps, as we have seen in some cases, more favourable economics encouraged others to take over. One wonders whether the reverse development from about 1970 in the South, where new independents began taking on routes abandoned by NBC, might be repeated later in the North.

It would be a pity if, as in some other parts of the country, bus services were allowed to get worse before they get better. There seems a reasonable chance that this will not happen, for two reasons, first, the continuing tradition of strong and vigorous management in many organisations of all sizes, and second in the influence of the Local Government Act, 1972. This ordained that County Councils should 'develop policies which will promote the provision of a co-ordinated and efficient system of public passenger transport to meet the needs of the county and, for that purpose, to take such steps to promote the co-ordination, amalgamation and reorganisation of road passenger transport undertakings as appear to the County Council to be desirable'; subsequent ministry circulars strongly suggested a transfer of expenditure from roads to support of public transport. It meant more, however, than the ad hoc

173

subsidies for unremunerative services that tended to arise out of the 1968 Act, in requiring a detailed examination of what the public needed, and many counties are building public transport teams on a scale unknown before. Independents seem likely to benefit from an undercurrent of sympathy towards them in the local authorities, not least in those of traditional socialist domination. Whereas one might expect a preference for state-owned public transport, there has often been a cry to 'bring in the private operator', and in the North East, unlike many other parts, there are indeed frequently independents awaiting the opportunity. There is also a requirement for local authorities to look at overall transport planning, including the need or otherwise for controls on private cars by traffic management schemes or parking restrictions in towns.

Uncertainty regarding their new rights and duties has led some shire counties to wonder whether their objects might best be achieved by direct ownership of bus fleets as in the metropolitan counties. Financial stringency seems likely to prevent large-scale expenditure in the near future, even if the counties were encouraged by central government to buy, but if, as seems probable, support for bus services becomes vastly more expensive in the coming years, there will be a natural temptation to cut the knot.

Many would see the logic of transferring public transport controlled by central government, and administered through independent traffic commissioners, to local authorities who know what would be needed and who would be paying a large part of the cost. It could be, therefore, that the existing framework of companies largely dating from the BET and Tilling area agreements of the 1920s will disappear. It is the author's hope that if this does happen, and in many ways it would be a regrettable step, a record will exist of those companies with their history and traditions such as has been secured for the pre-grouping railways.

APPENDIX

General Managers and Chief Officers of the Group Companies and Municipal undertakings in this volume

(A) Companies

United Automobile	1912–1929	E. B. Hutchinson
Services	1929–1934	H. P. Stokes
	1934–1959	A. T. Evans
	1959–1969	B. T. Pratt
	1969–1974	D. G. F. Rawlinson
	1974–	K. Holmes

Northern General	1913–1926	R. W. Cramp
Transport	1926–1936	J. Petrie
	1936–1954	G. W. Hayter
	1954–1968	J. W. Forster
	1968–1972	L. S. Higgins
	1972–1973	J. B. Hargreaves
	1973–	D. D. N. Graham

East Yorkshire	1926–1933	E. J. Lee (*joint managing director*)
Motor Services	1926–1931	J. S. Wills (*secretary and joint managing director*)
	1931–1933	R. H. Maxwell (*manager*)
	1933–1943	R. T. Ebrey
	1943–1974	C. R. H. Wreathall
	1974–1976	B. L. Rootham
	1976–	B. M. K. Horner

(B) Municipal Undertakings

Kingston-upon-Hull	1899–1919	W. J. M'Combe (*traffic manager*)
Corporation	1919–1931	E. S. Rayner
Transport	1931–1935	D. P. Morrison
	1935–1939	J. Lawson
	1939–1941	Interregnum
	1941–1965	G. H. Pulfrey
	1965–	W. K. Haigh

Newcastle Corporation Transport	1900–1905	A. E. Le Rossignol
	1905–1926	E. Hatton
	1926–1941	T. P. Easton
	1941–1946	H. C. Godsmark
	1947–1969	F. S. Taylor
	1969–	G. Stringer
South Shields Corporation Transport	1906–1908	J. Wilson
	1908–1912	L. E. Harvey
	1912–1915	W. T. Robson
	1915–1925	J. C. Whiteley
	1925–1934	J. A. Baker
	1934–1935	E. R. L. Fitzpayne
	1935–1937	H. Muscroft
	1937–1949	H. J. Troughton
	1949–1964	J. Crawford
	1964–1968	R. E. Bottrill
	1968–1969	J. M. Smith
Sunderland Corporation Transport	1900–1903	J. F. Snell (*chief electrical & tramways engineer*)
	1903–1929	A. R. Dayson
	1929–1948	C. A. Hopkins
	1948–1952	H. W. Snowball
	1952–1967	N. Morton
	1968–1969	R. E. Bottrill
	1969–1973	A. H. Wright

Tyneside Passenger Transport 1969–1975

Dr. T. M. Ridley (*director-general*)

Executive (Tyne & Wear PTE 1975–
From April 1974)   D. P. C. Fletcher (*director-general*)

Middlesbrough Corporation Transport	1921–1934	H. G. Jeken
	1934–1964	F. Lythgoe
	1964–1968	G. Stringer
Stockton Corporation Transport	1921–1933	Foster
	1933–1958	W. M. Campbell
	1958–1968	W. C. Wilson

Teesside Railless Traction Board	1921–1930	J. B. Parker
	1930–1955	C. W. F. Cozens
	1955–1968	W. Flynn

Teesside Municipal Transport

| (Cleveland Transit | 1968–1972 | W. C. Wilson |
| From April 1974) | 1972– | W. R. Holland |

Darlington Corporation Transport	1904–1937	J. R. P. Lunn
	1937–1950	W. H. Penman
	1950–1972	W. Mayes
	1972–	P. A. Ellis

West Hartlepool Corporation Transport	1911–1926	T. G. Richardson
	1926–1929	J. H. Parker
	1929–1931	H. E. Blackiston
	1931–1957	A. R. Burton
	1957–1960	A. Barlow
	1960–1964	R. E. Bottrill

| Hartlepool Corporation Transport | 1964–1972 | T. J. Sheppard |
| | 1972– | G. G. Fearnley |

BIBLIOGRAPHY AND ACKNOWLEDGEMENTS

For general bus history the only compact sources are L. A. G. Strong's *The Rolling Road* and, more recently, John Hibbs' *History of British Bus Services*. Local tramways are well represented by G. S. Hearse's *Histories* of the Gateshead, Jarrow and South Shields and Northumberland systems, and S. A. Staddon's *Tramways of Sunderland*, while there is reference to all of these in J. C. Gillham and W. H. Bett's *Great British Tramway Networks*. The railway background is covered by the two appropriate David & Charles Regional Histories, *Scotland – The Lowlands and Borders* by John Thomas, and *The North East* by Ken Hoole, who in his *North Eastern Railway Buses, Lorries and Autocars* gives more details of the NER's road interests.

Buses are not so well served; the only books on individual undertakings are Ron Howe's *Darlington Municipal Transport – Trams, Trolleys and Buses*, the commemorative booklets published by Newcastle and Sunderland Corporations on their transfer to the PTE, and chapters on Wright Bros, Economic and York Pullman in K. L. Turns' *The Independent Bus*. There is also material in Roger Fulford's history of British Electric Traction, and I have made use of an unpublished source in R. W. Malins' MSc thesis at Durham University 'The Busmen: A Study of Industrial Relations in Two Bus Companies in the North-East of England' (1972). Fortunately there are many relevant Omnibus Society publications, notably on Durham District Services, East Yorkshire, Northern Independent Bus Operators, and the Small Stage Carriage Operators of Yorkshire.

A good deal of history is available in periodicals, of which *Bus and Coach*, *Buses*, *Coaching Journal*, *Commercial Motor*, the *Leyland Journal*, *Motor Transport*, and the *Omnibus Magazine* contribute much over the years. Most important and valuable of all was the help and information willingly given by officers of the companies, municipalities and Tyne & Wear PTE.

Many independent operators, too, went out of their way to assist, of whom perhaps especially Fyfe Gillett, Charles Marshall and Robert Tait should be mentioned. (At the same time I should emphasise that the resulting book is in no way an official history of any business, nor does it represent the views of its management.)

I also acknowledge with gratitude the contributions made by numerous other organisations and individuals, among them The Omnibus Society, The Northern Group Enthusiasts' Club, the Durham County Planning Officer, Charles Klapper, Douglas Mennear and Newcastle Polytechnic, without whose facilities and indulgence in many ways the exercise would have been impossible, and not least Mrs. V. Holding, for cheerfully undertaking all the typing.

INDEX

GENERAL INDEX

181

INDEX OF BUS AND COACH OPERATORS

183